Developing Strategies and Practices for Culturally Diverse Classrooms

Developing Strategies and Practices for Culturally Diverse Classrooms

Joyce Taylor Gibson

Christopher-Gordon Publishers, Inc.
Norwood, Massachusetts

Credits

Every effort has been made to contact copyright holders for permission to reproduce borrowed material where necessary. We apologize for any oversights and will be happy to rectify them in future printings.

Stages of Concern Process, used by permission. Hall, G. E., and Hord, S. M. (1987). *Change in Schools Facilitating the Process*. Albany, NY: State University of New York Press.

The Bill Harp Professional Teacher's Library
An Imprint of
Christopher-Gordon Publishers, Inc.
1502 Providence Highway, Suite #12
Norwood, MA 02062
(800) 934-8322

Printed in the United States of America

10 9 8 7 6 5 4 3 2 1   04 03 02 01 00 99

Library of Congress Catalog Card Number: 98-073520
ISBN: 0-926842-87-0

Dedication

This book is dedicated to my parents, Thelma Bernice Taylor and Jeremiah Alexander Taylor, who gave me my first lessons in diversity.

Acknowledgments

Several people have guided me through the creation of this book. I am indebted to them all.

First, for offering me the opportunity to write this book, I thank my mentor and colleague Professor Bill Harp, whose encouragement and support have been critical for its completion. Those talented, anonymous reviewers who read my early drafts are angels in disguise; their feedback was always useful, and contributed to the quality of the manuscript. Students from my diversity classes brought new meaning and insights for this book throughout the years as we have learned from each other.

Finally, I am especially thankful for my resident editor and partner Roland, who always found time to lift my spirits in loving ways and to read just one more page.

Contents

INTRODUCTION

Developing Strategies and Practices for Culturally Diverse Classrooms is written for educators who are committed to working successfully with the diverse learners in our schools today. Learning to teach in culturally diverse classrooms does not happen immediately after your first course on children's learning styles, or your last history course on minorities in the United States. And it does not happen just because you finally arranged a team teaching schedule with the special needs teacher for your third grade class.

Learning to teach in culturally diverse classrooms does not simply kick in after a particular event or educational epiphany! It is akin to learning a new language. Both require a process and practice for fluency. You begin by learning the vocabulary, the sounds of the language, the culture and history of the people who speak the language. Then you learn the rules and guidelines for speaking and writing; and you learn to conjugate verbs and how to use words in appropriate contexts. And you practice. Your confidence grows as you learn to think and speak and write more fluently in the new language. You make progress and you make mistakes, but you keep studying. You create opportunities to learn more about native speakers, their customs and community rituals. And you practice. You visit local communities to practice, and become familiar with the sounds and uses of your new language. You even schedule your vacation in countries or communities where the language is spoken. And you continue to practice. You are becoming more skilled with the language, and in a few years you are fluent. Language instructors tell you what you already understand more fully now—you must use your new language, or lose it.

Becoming culturally competent in the classroom is similar to learning a new language, because it, too, requires a process. You must learn the vocabulary, the sounds and cultural perspectives of the children and their families. Understanding the history and current status of cultural groups will help you make more informed decisions about how to educate their children. Then you learn the norms and social structures of these micro-cultures, or neighborhoods, and how they impact the macro-culture, or the general society. And you practice by meeting the individuals and families who represent the children in your schools. Meeting family members must happen for greater mutual understanding. Your confidence grows as you begin to create new strategies to enhance the achievement of every child in your classroom. You make progress and you make mistakes, but you keep studying and learning. You create opportunities to interact with students and their families more and more as you become fluent in negotiating across cultures. As you journey toward cultural competence, practicing negotiating across cultures is absolutely necessary to remain adept. So, you practice, practice, practice.

Learning a language and becoming culturally competent require a commitment to study and practice, reflection about the learning process, openness to feedback, and a willingness to collaborate with others. In this book, I (1) define diversity and describe its implications for the teaching and learning process for educators in schools today, (2) offer a unique process for developing strategies to serve diverse populations, and (3) provide opportunities to practice the approach through questions, exercises, and scenarios. This book was written to enhance your understanding of diversity, and to make you more comfortable with what it means for your classroom and school. If you want to be more *conscious* of what you are already doing to teach students with different needs, and you want to become more skilled at working with children from different cultures, then this is written for you. It is a staff development primer designed to influence your thinking about how you can respond to the increasing diversity in your schools and classrooms.

My goal is to provide a process for you to ultimately create your own strategies and practices to positively influence the achievement of children from diverse cultures in your school. This process is designed to teach you how to consciously develop strategies and practices for cultural groups that are at risk of educational failure. The experience of other practitioners will be cited, but a major goal is to provide a process to support the development of strategies and practices **to fit the needs of your classroom or school**. *No one can do this better than you and a team of colleagues in your school.*

Chapter Review

Chapter 1, **What Does Diversity Mean?**, defines diversity, and describes historical and current research on the evolution of diverse students at risk of educational failure. For the ultimate concern in education is not about diversity itself, but the impact that differences have on how children achieve in schools. As you begin reading this book, I ask you to be open to learning without thinking of *your* perspective as the right one or standard by which other cultures are judged. When seeking to understand people different from yourself it is important to know that your idea of normal is just that—your idea of normal; other people's idea of normal may be altogether different, based on their cultural perspective.

Martin Haberman (1993), who writes about how middle-class values are the assessment guide for determining what is normal for two- and three-year-old urban children, could be speaking to all of us when he speaks of how we have stretched and imposed the meaning of normal beyond its original meaning: "The word normal which began with the meaning of 'frequently observed' is thus changed into 'behavior considered healthy'" (p. 2). So new teachers and others tend to view what the middle-class two- and three-year-olds do as normal, meaning desirable behavior; and what any other two- and three-year-olds do as undesirable, or not normal. Haberman (1993) rejects this interpretation and helps us regain our perspective:

> Children develop by interacting with specific people
> in particular environments. What is "normal" in one

set of circumstances will not be normal in another. In fact, given the facts of life in growing up in urban poverty today it is clearly unreasonable to expect children to resemble textbook models future teachers are trained to regard as normal. The important point is that the urban poor are quite normal. *They are making perfectly reasonable responses to those who raise them and to the life conditions under which they live and grow.* (p. 2)

As you read this book, I urge you to make the effort to understand the environment and circumstances that children in at-risk situations experience, before making assumptions and judgments based on your own experience. You will then be better prepared to move forward to assist a child, no matter the environment—be it urban, rural, or suburban. In this chapter you will also find a review of the goals of education in a democratic society and how these ideas can affect teaching and learning with diverse students.

Chapter 2, **Diversity and Culture**, takes you into the interconnecting worlds of culture—those of the children you serve, and your own. Culture is defined through describing specific *ways of being* unique to certain groups, as well as those *ways of being* we share in common as members of the American society. You are introduced to the work of Dr. Mel Levine, an educator and professor of pediatrics, who believes that the negative labeling and separation of children is often more harmful than the learning problems they experience. He offers a caring perspective for children with learning problems that promotes collaboration and inclusion, instead of separation, which he believes almost always carries with it a lifetime of stigmatization. His exceptional book, *Educational Care: A System for Understanding and Helping Children with Learning Problems at Home and School,* is a compelling resource that enhances our work with *any* child, but especially those with learning problems.

Chapter 3, **Beliefs, Pedagogy, and Change**, offers a description of four critical areas for teachers to use to analyze their progress in developing cultural competence: (1) beliefs and knowledge about diverse groups, (2) reflections on pedagogical practices, (3) understanding your personal response to the change process, and (4) building networks and resources to support your work. These four areas define a process for using the ideas from the first two chapters, and constitute the major ways I believe practitioners can accommodate human differences in the classroom. Belief is such a powerful factor in how we behave that it transcends data, performance, or any other reality that offers us information about students. Therefore, an examination of your belief system is critical to understanding how to behave toward students different from you. Our beliefs are reflected through our instructional practices, which is one way students can discern our relationship with them. Examination of our instructional practices may lead to changes to support learners in new ways; understanding how you respond to making changes is important as you work toward the goals for each child. Distinguishing your response to change from your response to the new practice itself is important in helping you evaluate your efforts toward the goal.

The last section in this chapter presents a model of how teachers view change, and demonstrates how building networks with colleagues and members of the community can be useful in working with children from diverse cultures.

Chapter 4, **Diversity and Achievement**, presents a topic of great concern to all teachers—student achievement. Are children from diverse backgrounds capable of academic gains in spite of their lack of fluency in English; their physical and mental problems; their economic, racial, and environmental challenges? And are you capable of teaching them? Concerns about the intelligence of diverse students is tackled in this chapter, along with a section on how teachers' expectations can make children winners or losers in the educational system.

Chapter 5, **Moving Toward Cultural Competence**, describes several scenarios that provide opportunities for teachers to develop strategies and techniques for children at risk of educational failure. I will walk with you through a couple of the scenarios, analyzing them by using appropriate aspects of the process described in Chapter 3. Your job is to use your own experience, add ideas from this book that appeal to you, and direct your own resources toward resolution of the scenario. This chapter lays the groundwork for you to enter the formal planning for a specific Action Plan to try in your classroom or school. The instructions for your Action Plan are described in Chapter 6.

Chapter 6, **Planning for Diversity in Classrooms and Schools,** launches you into a future of exciting planning for reaching very specific goals concerning the human diversity represented by students in your classroom and school. Working on your own goals for a specific challenge with one or a group of your children is the goal of chapter. Looking back at the concepts and strategies in the preceding five chapters, you will find that each is unique, yet connected to all the other ideas presented, and together they constitute a journey toward cultural competence.

There are summary questions at the end of each chapter to stimulate your thinking about the human diversity in your classrooms. I strongly recommend that you use this book as a staff development resource, and that you work with at least one other colleague on this journey toward cultural competence. Following the summary questions, there is a **Diversity Notebook**, a place where exercises and resources are described for your use. It is also a place for your notes and questions. Now, turn the page to begin your journey.

References

Haberman, M. (1993). Contexts: Overview and Framework. In M. J. O'Hara and S. J. Odell (Eds.), *Diversity and teaching: Teacher education yearbook I* (p. 2) Fort Worth, TX: HarcourtBrace Jovanovich College Publishers.

Levine, M. (1994). *Educational care: A system for understanding and helping children with learning problems—at home and in school*. Cambridge, MA: Educuators Publishing Service, Inc.

CHAPTER 1

What Does Diversity Mean?

Diversity means difference. The Longman Language Activator also defines diversity this way: "of various kinds" (1994, p. 364). But what kinds of differences do you mean when referring to diversity in your school? The meaning of diversity is not as universal as some people would have you believe. Therefore, it is very important that you define diversity whenever you use it, and that you describe the context in which you are using it. Ask others to offer you the same courtesy when they refer to diversity in schools.

I define diversity in schools in a very particular way. To provide context for your understanding of my definition, I invite you to join me in observing the first day of a class for pre-service students. We are observing through the inner thoughts of the professor:

She enters the large room ten minutes before the class begins, and notices that several students have already arrived. Some are standing around the table, talking casually, while a few others are sitting, examining the texts for the class. She smiles, nods to greet them, and proceeds to set up for the class.

It is a sunny fall day, the shades are up, and the room is full of light. There is energy and anticipation in the air. She thinks to herself, "This is my seventh year teaching this course, and each time I am still excited about how the class will handle the material. I wonder what kinds of relationships we will develop with each other, and how many are really interested and committed to working to help *all* the children achieve at high levels." More students arrive since it is almost time for class to begin.

"Most of them look so young, not like graduate students, but more like junior or senior undergraduates. There are, however, a few older students, close to my age—women returning to school after raising families, and others changing careers most likely. They usually bring depth and balance to our discussions just from their years of life experience. It is good to have them in class interacting with the younger students. 'Good afternoon, class'; I hope you are all here for the course, *Diversity in the Classroom*. We are ready to begin." They exchange pleasantries about the first week of classes, and then she asks **the question.** They look surprised at first, wondering, she imagines, why she is asking such an obvious question. A few students raise their hands, but she ignores them, and repeats the question: **"Why do you think the College requires pre-service teachers to take this course, 'Diversity in the Classroom'?"**

They begin to respond, at first tentatively. She calls on one of the students who had her hand up earlier.

"The national teaching force is predominately white, and the student population is increasingly children of color; new teachers need to know more about the cultures of these new students." She motions to a young man near the woman who answered first.

"New teachers need to learn more about the different learning styles of their students, regardless of their race or culture."

"These are good answers. Let me hear from someone on the other side of the room."

"As teachers we have to understand how to get along with people from all walks of life, and a course like this will help us do that." An older student answers now: *"Many people in our society are prejudiced and still treat some groups unfairly, even in schools; we need to understand more about how to protect children from these practices."*

"These are appropriate answers, and it seems you are already attuned to some of the issues for some diverse populations. Can you think of any other reasons to offer this course? Take five minutes and discuss the question with folks at your tables." After five minutes, they begin again, and only one student is waving her hand to be called on. *"My father's a teacher, and I remember his telling me that the state required him to know more about different kinds of students to satisfy his certification requirement."*

"That's correct, the state does require new teachers to know how to work with different types of students, be they linguistic minorities, special needs children, or children from racial and economic minorities."

The professor is pleased, but not quite satisfied. She asks the question another way, to engender deeper thinking. "What do you know about the status of special needs children, sub-dominant and poor children in this state and in our country that would influence a College of Education to offer this course?" They are quiet again, searching for the answer. When the wait time becomes too uncomfortable for them, she begins to answer softly, at first, and slowly, walking carefully, making eye contact as she utters every word, her voice growing louder and more serious until she finishes and stands rigidly and silently before them:

> THESE CHILDREN ARE SOME OF THE MOST UNDERPREPARED IN OUR SCHOOLS, THE POTENTIAL DROP OUTS, THE PULL OUTS, THE MOST LIKELY TO BE ABSENT OR PLACED IN SPECIAL EDUCATION OR TO BE IN THE LOW READING GROUPS. THEY SCORE THE LOWEST ON STANDARDIZED TESTS, ARE DISCIPLINED MORE THAN OTHER STUDENTS; THEY ARE THE MOST LIKELY TO BE REFERRED TO VOCATIONAL EDUCATION PROGRAMS, THE LEAST LIKELY TO FEEL CONFIDENT IN THEMSELVES, AND THE MOST LIKELY TO FEEL THAT TEACHERS DO NOT CARE ABOUT THEM. THEY ARE RARELY CONSIDERED GIFTED, ARE USUALLY TRACKED TO THE LEAST RIGOROUS PROGRAMS, AND ARE OFTEN WITHOUT FAMILY ADVOCATES TO SUPPORT THEM.

The students are very quiet now. And she continues:

> IN OTHER WORDS, THESE CHILDREN ARE THE MOST LIKELY TO BE AT RISK OF FAILING IN OUR SCHOOLS. AT A TIME WHEN CHILDREN WITH THESE CHARACTERISTICS ARE INCREASING IN OUR SCHOOLS, SOME EDUCATORS ARE CLAIMING THAT THE CHILDREN ARE AT FAULT. IN OTHER WORDS, THE CHILDREN ARE THE PROBLEM. I SUGGEST THAT YOU CONSIDER ANOTHER

VIEW—THAT THESE ARE ACTUALLY ADULT PROBLEMS—YOURS
AND MINE, AND PROBLEMS OF OTHER ADULTS—ADULTS IN THE
COMMUNITY AND ADULTS IN FAMILIES.

"You are in this course to learn how to solve adult problems
for children who are failing or at risk of failing in schools. Too many
of our children are at risk of failing in school, and their failing
drags us down as a profession, as a society, as a nation. Is it coinci-
dental that the majority are students of color, minority, or oppressed
groups in our society?

"As educators, you must always think *first* about the learning
questions, not about the child's race, gender, or handicap, despite
the fact that you may notice those things first. Ask the learning
questions: Why isn't this student participating in class? Or, what
are the obstacles that get in the way when these students try to
learn? To what can I attribute these poor grades? Are there school
factors that contribute to his lack of motivation? Why is it so difficult for her to turn in her homework?

"Yes, there is discrimination and racism, and yes, we do need
to know about different learning styles of children. However, your
primary focus is the teaching/learning process. Too often educators
get caught up in focusing on unfair treatment to the *exclusion* of
the question of whether the child is *growing academically*. Of para-
mount importance is your understanding of your primary goals as
teachers." The professor's final words before inviting the students
to comment on her oration were:

"Be clear about your commitment to each child and how your
goals fit with the goals of the school. Staying focused on these academic goals will serve you well as you unravel what gets in the way
of student achievement. I suggest that we analyze the problem for
each different group, in the context of their respective environments;
then we can ask questions before we make recommendations for
improvement."

What are *your* questions about the professor's approach of
defining diversity in the context of achievement, or, more specifically, educational failure?

Before answering, please indicate in the spaces below at least
three groups you thought about as the instructor described the students at risk of failing. (1) _____
(2) _____ (3) _____.

If you listed special needs children, included accelerated learners, those with behavioral problems, or those with mental deficiencies, girls, children with physical handicaps, poor children, or second language learners, then you already have some idea of my definition of diversity. Many children in these categories are at risk in some unique ways in classrooms and schools systems across our country. Before providing a formal definition, though, I would like you to take a look into some classrooms for more specifics about diversity. If you believe there is an issue of diversity in the scenarios below, make a **check plus (+)** in the space provided. If you believe there is not an issue of diversity, place a **check minus (–)** in the space provided.

A. In a suburban town an hour's drive from a major inner city, the school population is no longer predominately white; close to 55 percent are a mix of African American, Cambodian, Chinese, Portuguese, and Hispanic, primarily Dominican. The teachers are predominately white in all the schools (elementary, middle and secondary), and there has been a growing division among them about how to address their concerns about the different behaviors of the students, in class and out. None of the new diverse groups is enrolled in higher-level or college-bound programs, except the Chinese, and the racial incidents and misunderstandings among students and staff seem to increase each year. Parents of the new students have complained of the unfair treatment their children have received in class and during extra-curricular activities. Tension is high among staff, and there seems to be little leadership provided by principals or the school committee regarding their concerns. Do diversity issues exist? _____

B. A Black elementary school teacher in an inner-city school is distressed to learn that the parents of the two white children and the three Arab American children have asked for a meeting to discuss concerns about their children's academic progress. The 20 other children in her class are Black. She wonders how these families came together, and what these "concerns" are. Later she learns from the principal that one of the concerns of the families is about accelerated, or gifted, programs for their children; at least one family has discussed transferring out of the school if these programs cannot be provided. Do diversity issues exist? _____

C. In a small island community, elementary and middle school children attend school together. The town has 100 year-round families, and only about half have young children. When children reach high school age, they have to take the ferry to a regional school serving the island and coastal towns. Last year two jet ski accidents severely injured two children from different families; one sustained head injuries, the other is paralyzed from the waist down, but perhaps not permanently. In the meantime, the families and the school staff have made every effort to accommodate the needs of the children for school, but no one on staff has experience in special education. New state inclusion laws require that all children be educated together, which means there are to be no more pullouts. The trauma of the accident seems to have affected both children academically, but they have never been tested. Teachers and family members are concerned about their school progress, and how to prepare for their futures. The school committee has heard only negative reports about the potential costs of arranging services to meet their needs. Do diversity issues exist? _____

How did you check the three scenarios? If you chose a **check +** for each scenario, then you probably understand more about the various kinds of diversity than you might have imagined. Diversity is not just about race, second language learners, or people who look different from you. Diversity means difference, and there are many differences found in the human condition. These three scenarios should raise many questions in your mind about the variety of diversity issues facing school personnel each day. All the issues are certainly not depicted here. I will share a particular perspective with you, in hopes that it will prepare you to address any diversity issue you many encounter. So let us begin with *my* definition.

Defining Diversity

I define diversity quite broadly: It means human differences. Human differences may be visible physical features and behaviors, or invisible ideas, concepts, or activities that are extraordinary in our personal or professional experience. Extraordinary in terms of what is considered the mainstream, or just unusual in the context or environment in which the behavior or activity is noticed. This is a book designed to challenge educators' thinking about the most effective ways to teach children regardless of their human differences, and to enhance educators' knowledge about the enormous capacity for learning that all children possess. More important, it is about the ***untapped power, the sense of personal efficacy*** that teachers must demonstrate to help prevent more children from failing in school and in life. Far too many children never experience the joy of learning or understand their potential for achievement and success in life. As educators we must ignite the fire for learning and instill the hope and confidence in each child that success can be achieved. We must demonstrate that if we use our unique capacity to think and solve problems, which is shared by no other creature in the animal kingdom, each one of us has the opportunity to live a quality life and make worthy contributions to our democratic society.

Diversity understood as human differences gives us common ground for communication. We are all human beings, despite certain differences, some of which could be called cultural in the sense that we have a distinct way of doing things that is understood primarily by the group with which we associate; but not so foreign as to not be understandable by others. After all, what we share in common in our society is not insignificant, especially if we look at our connections as Americans. Most groups are here because they wanted the freedoms we share as a result of the way we are governed; our rights of expression, assembly, or worship, of due process when in difficulty; our national pastimes—sports and entertainment; and that ubiquitous vehicle of cultural continuity—television. We have only to look at our national, annual rituals that show how we are connected: school starting dates, national holidays, summer vacations, tax due dates, voting days, just to mention a few. A general theme in this book is the emphasis on our common ground, as humans, as Americans, living in a democracy. For I believe that our greatest problems arise when we take for granted, ignore, or forget our common ground, and focus almost exclusively on our differences, usually to the detriment of our mission as educators.

Reactions to Human Differences

Educators often respond adversely to human differences in children's behaviors or conditions because they are (a) responding emotionally at the moment, (b) just following procedure, (c) unaware of their negative impact on the child, (d) conditioned by stereotypes to respond a certain way, or (e) simply not thinking of the **best interests of the child** at that time. Their thinking is generated by what social psychologist Jeff Howard (1991) calls "other influences" or distractions that prevent them from focusing on their professional roles as educators. In this frame of mind, teachers often shift their responsibility to others: "If only parents would do a better job of preparing these kids." Peter Negroni, superintendent of the Springfield, Massachusetts, public schools regularly tells audiences that "parents send us the best children they have!" (Presentation at conference, 1994).

Unfortunately, in many school communities, teachers and other educators are not accepting of all children as learners, and do not understand them or what they need to succeed in school. And though there are few standard or universal professional development programs that address the broad face of human differences, the good news is that most of the challenges of human differences are **manageable** and **solvable**—by committed educators. By using this primer, educators can learn to respond more effectively to children who represent human differences in a variety of ways.

Children At Risk of Educational Failure

The *1994 Report on Education Reforms and Students At Risk: A Review of the Current State of the Art* is a comprehensive resource that documents the history and current research on children at risk in our society. It also describes in detail the national programs and initiatives that are operating to help children at risk. One section is particularly pertinent to our topic, and provides a context for defining those groups I will be discussing in this book:

> Historically, separate and unequal schooling has limited the educational opportunities of poor children and children of color. In addition, these children sometimes have problems outside school that interfere with learning. Hunger, poor health, high mobility, homelessness, violence—these are just a few of the problems that many young people face in impoverished urban and rural areas. (p. 2)

These are societal problems that children bring to schools. Other institutions and agencies beyond the schools can and should be working with educators to help manage these conditions while children are trying to learn. Yet children themselves often bear the brunt of blame for their circumstances:

> They must also confront a less tangible threat—the devaluation of their talents and potential. They are labeled "problem children" or the "special needs population," implying they are somehow intrinsically less intelligent, more needy. But sufficient food, shelter, health care, and schooling are basic, not "special" needs, and cultural differences become a problem only when we fail to address diversity honestly and fairly. (p. 2)

Adults at home, in our communities and in schools, as well as in our other institutions are the ones who devalue these children, *our* children. Children cannot devalue themselves without an adult having done it to them first! A final note about the broad sweep of diverse children at risk of failure is provided by the following passage:

> Poor children and children of color are not the only students at risk. Perhaps more than at any other time in the nation's history, schools are being asked to recognize and address the needs of children who suffer from emotional problems, abuse, or neglect. Schools are also increasingly aware that low social status may depress student performance regardless of family

> income: Recent studies, for example, describe the
> ways in which girls may be discouraged from pursu-
> ing male-dominated professions. And the media
> seems to remind us daily that academic mediocrity
> may place all U.S. students at risk of being unable to
> compete in global markets. (p. 3)

Groups not referred to specifically here are children who have handicaps, are English language learners, or children uncertain about
their sexual orientation, as well as those children who may have
some combination of these characteristics. Many of us want to believe that the students at risk reside only in low-income neighborhoods, and that they are only those of the sub-dominant groups in
our society. As this national report attests and other research sup-
ports, though there may be a heavier incidence of certain types of
risks among poor people, other risks can be found across income
levels and among dominant and sub-dominant groups.

   This discussion about children who manifest human differences that place them at risk of educational failure raises the question of how teachers approach any child as a learner. First
impressions can lead any of us to erroneous assumptions or faulty
conclusions. But we can easily recover from those first impressions
by setting up a means to assess what each child brings as a learner
at the first meeting. By withholding final judgment, we allow ourselves to observe and to ask questions of the child, former teachers,
and the parents—and begin to learn the real strengths and weaknesses in a child's development. Such a balanced assessment helps
a teacher design a plan of action appropriate for each learner.

How Can We Address These Challenges?

The recent Report of the National Commission on Teaching and
America's Future (1996) declared that "A caring, competent, and
qualified teacher *for every child* is the most important ingredient
in education reform . . . **students are entitled to teachers who
know their subjects, *understand their students and what they
need*, and have developed the skills required to make learning come alive**" [Emphasis added] (Executive Summary, p. 6).
Educational reform is necessary when the goals of schooling are

not being met at local and national levels. Diversity must be recognized and addressed, but not at the expense of the goals of education. They cannot be separate.

Our diversity is our strength, and it must not detract from our basic goals of schooling. Our Constitution delegates the responsibility of education to the states and the people, and for many an education is the best means to access that quality life that is so illusive in other parts of the world and in many corners of our own society. We cannot deliberately ignore or unconsciously abdicate our responsibility because someone looks or behaves different from the majority.

Goodlad (1996) in Soder's book *Democracy, Education and the Schools,* reminds us of the central purpose of schooling in the United States: "The mission of schooling comes down to two related kinds of enculturation: no other institution is so charged. The first is for political and social responsibility as a citizen. The second is for maximum individual development, for full participation in the human conversation (with the concept of conversations expanded into a metaphor for the whole of daily living)" (p. 112). I believe the assumption that we operate under in democratic schools has led to some of the problems we actually have with addressing the needs of diverse populations. Teaching about democratic schools does not necessarily happen in teacher education programs, nor are its ideals practiced by personnel in schools simply because we live in a democratic society.

These concepts flow out of the philosophy of John Dewey (1916), who believed that people in a democracy ought to be taught how to live democratically, and that one of the best places to learn how to live democratically is in the schools. How to do that in today's school is a significant challenge. Though often difficult to define, Apple and Beane (1995) offer persuasive ideas about what the conditions of a "democratic way of life" might look like in education, for children and adults:

1. The open flow of ideas, regardless of their popularity, that enables people to be as fully informed as possible.

2. Faith in the individual and collective capacity of people to create possibilities for resolving problems.

3. The use of critical reflection and analysis to evaluate ideas, problems, and policies.

4. Concern for the welfare of others and "the common good."

5. Concern for the dignity and rights of individuals and minorities.

6. An understanding that democracy is not so much an "ideal" to be pursued as an "idealized" set of values that we must live and that must guide our life as a people.

7. The organization of social institutions to promote and extend the democratic way of life. (pp. 6, 7)

These ideas raise questions some of us have not considered seriously since we first joined the profession, or since our last professional development experience. It is this level of consciousness about your professional goals and responsibility as teachers that I want you to be clear about—as much as possible on a daily basis. Being conscientious at this level will help you understand why you do what you do for any child, no matter what challenges he or she brings to you that day. It is when we get lost in the pressures of everyday tasks and demands that we lose perspective; thus when things don't seem right, it is easy to focus on the areas where we often feel most vulnerable and least confident.

Children with human differences are too often those who represent the subdominant, oppressed groups, or simply those viewed as less valuable in our society. Thus socio-economic status, gender, and physical and mental handicaps are also factors, like race and language, that place children at risk of achieving well or of failing in our schools. Remembering and respecting our history as a democratic nation can support our efforts to educate all children well. By creating and sustaining democratic classrooms and schools, we implement a strategy for moving toward the goal of greater achievement for all, while benefiting ourselves and students. Acting and teaching democratically necessarily reinforces our work at high levels with all students.

What I am proposing in this book is an *internally* driven staff development process that will enhance your current efforts or help you create new venues to support greater achievement for all children. For when you improve life for the ones in difficulty, you necessarily improve life for everyone. To do this, educators must define the common ground shared with students and families to learn how to address the diversity challenges in schools. To do this, educators must define the common ground they share with students and families to learn how to address the diversity challenges in schools. Chapter 2, **Diversity and Culture,** provides the basis for examining commonalities among these groups.

Summary Questions
What Does Diversity Mean?

A.   Am I specific when I make references to human differences, instead of making assumptions that others understand my use of diversity?

B.   Am I able to describe a child at risk of failing with words and a tone that is caring and respectful of him or her as a valuable member of my class?

C.   Have I set up a climate in my classroom that fosters respectful and fair interactions for each of my students?

D.   Which of my lesson plans or activities this week reflected some of the democratic values I believe in?

Diversity Notebook

This is the first page of your **Diversity Notebook**, a section at the end of each chapter designed to trigger further thinking about the concepts, research, and practices described in the text. Questions are reflective of the major areas in each chapter and serve as ways to study the material further. There will be reminders, exercises, and some additional suggestions about what you can do to improve your skills for working with diverse students. It is also a place for *your* notes, musings, and questions; a place to keep a journal of your thoughts as you work through the process to improve outcomes for all students.

1. What type of diversity (human differences) can you identify in your classroom? In your school?

2. Can you identify the children at risk of failing in your classroom?

    a. What type of diversity is represented in this group?
    b. Are they similar or different from children at risk of failing in your school?
    c. What teaching strategies are you employing now to address the students at risk of failing?

3. Do you know enough history about the diverse groups in your classroom to aid your understanding about their current status?

4. Draft a statement describing your goals for your students. Share it with your peers, and then find out how close your goals are to the school's mission. Discuss your findings with your peers.

5. Are you willing to work with a team of peers to support greater learning to serve the diverse needs of your diverse students?

    a. What role(s) can you play with the group?
    b. Which group of diverse learners do you want to teach more effectively?

Review one of the scenarios on pages 5–6 and generate questions you might ask to begin the discussions about how to overcome the challenges to achievement in the communities described. List the questions below. You can refer to them later when we discuss the cases in Chapter 4.

Share the conditions of a "democratic way of life" described by Apple and Beane with a colleague, and discuss whether you recognize those that may be present in your classroom or schools.

References

Apple, M., & Beane, J. A. (Eds.). (1995). *Democratic schools.* Alexandria, VA: Association for Supervision and Curriculum Development.

Banks, J. A., & Banks, C. A. (1997). *Multicultural education: Issues and perspectives.* Boston: Allyn and Bacon.

Department of Education (1994). *Education reforms and students at risk: A review of the current state of the art.* Washington, DC: Author. Internet at http://www.ed.gov/pubs/EdReformstudies/EdReforms/

Dewey, J. (1916). *Democracy and education.* New York: Macmillan.

Goodlad, J. (1996). Democracy, education and community. In R. Soder, (Ed.), *Democracy, education and the schools* (p. 112). San Francisco: Jossey-Bass.

Howard, J. (1991). Efficacy Institute training manual. Lexington, MA: The Efficacy Institute.

Schaefer, R. T. (1990). *Racial and ethnic groups.* New York: HarperCollins.

Spring, J. (1997). *Deculturalization and the struggle for equality: A history of the education of dominated cultures in the United States.* New York: McGraw-Hill.

CHAPTER 2

Diversity and Culture

In this chapter the reader will learn about the interconnecting worlds of culture. Each of us belongs to a primary culture, yet we have many things in common. This second step in learning to be culturally competent offers us a means with which to examine these cultural world views and find where the connections are with people in our school communities.

As educators we grapple with complex cultural and demographic changes while we attempt to stay attuned to developments in the field that help us to better meet the needs of all students. As children mature under the care of their parents or adult caretakers at home, educators are expected to learn and understand more about the cultural world view or cultural domain in which the children live. Children's cultural views may be unique in some ways, but they will also have aspects that we recognize from the larger macro-culture, our common society. Because we are citizens living in a democratic society, common ways of life have evolved through the injustice and struggle that define us and bind us as Americans, such as our freedoms of speech, assembly, and religion; these are examples of our large social system or macro-culture. The compulsory educational laws in our country can also be counted as a component of the macro-culture. Our cultural distinctions are our sub-systems or micro-cultures, which are influenced by our families, friends, and neighbors, as well as the local culture and values determined by the region, county, town, or city where we live.

My training in cultural anthropology heavily influences my definition of culture. Harry Wolcott (1976), a well-known anthropologist, suggests that "... anthropologists view culture as process, recognizing that it is ongoing, elusive, and always being modified ... The anthropologist is duty-bound to look at cultural patterns and cultural forms shared by members of a social system or sub system" (p. 24). For our work together, this idea of looking at culture as process, ongoing, ever-changing, is important in understanding how so many groups of people in the United States co-exist even though their histories and world views may be dissimilar. The distinguishing aspects of the "American" common way of life co-exist with multiple cultural distinctions.

Cultural pluralism, or acculturation, implies that there is mutual respect between and among cultural groups, without the discrimination, hostility, and prejudice that many groups have historically suffered while evolving in our society (Schaefer, 1990). Cultural pluralism does not exist yet in America. Many individuals and groups are working toward it as a goal, while other individuals and groups are working to prevent a pluralistic culture in the United States. Schools, by definition, are engaged in this conversation, and educators need to understand the importance of this issue simply on a factual basis. Increasingly, our society and all our schools are more diverse, and these trends will continue into the 21st century. I believe we have a moral responsibility to educate all children well—something that has eluded our society thus far. The historical record in America is replete with examples of discrimination, hostility, and injustice experienced by individuals and groups who were denied the basic Constitutional rights of "life, liberty and the pursuit of happiness," simply because they were "different" from the dominant culture. I believe we must *acknowledge* the historical discrepancies and injustices experienced by dominated groups in our society, but not waste energy denying they happened or feeling guilty about them—we cannot change history. However, we can channel that energy into not repeating or perpetuating injustices, and we can use it instead to prepare all the children to achieve at high levels, expecting them to succeed and lead successful lives.

Defining Culture

Every adult has a culture and operates within a culture, some-times several simultaneously. Adults are the primary caretakers of children and are usually the ones who transmit and interpret the culture to them. As children learn the habits, traditions, and ways of life of their families, they accept them as the way to do things whether at home or at school, yet they are cognizant of the differ-ences in their primary cultural domain and that of others. Each of us operates primarily out of a dominant cultural domain, some-times two, but there is usually an identifiable "way of being" that we as groups and individuals follow in the roles we play in our lives. My definition of culture is an amalgam of my own ideas and the ideas of others I have read over the years: **a way of life, a way of being and doing things that is understood by a particular group of people, whose ways are distinct from other groups** (Banks & Banks, 1997; Roberts, 1976; Wolcott, 1976). Cultures are influenced by the environment, but are not necessarily defined by them.

   People take their cultures with them, incorporate new ways of being, drop others, yet can retain some original ways of being as long as there are connections to others who uphold them. This is usually done by adults passing ways of being on to the next genera-tion, as well as reinforcing them with each other. There are many places in our country where cultures overlap or interconnect, cre-ating our unique pluralistic American culture. **I believe we must examine first what we share in common—the macro-systems—then consider those elements that make our cul-tures unique—the micro-systems.**

   A look, for example, at culturally distinct neighborhoods may have as much to do with people wanting to live together because they have familial and cultural bonds as it does with economics or discrimination. The Italian, Haitian, Greek, Irish, and Cambodian neighborhoods exist in part because people can function better in a community when they know the customs and language and tradi-tions—even though they are all Americans! If America is the macro-culture or largest social system, then ethnic, racial, or other group distinctions are micro-cultures, or sub-systems of the larger sys-tem. Most people learn to co-exist in several micro-cultures or sub-systems while functioning in the wider macro-culture. I like to think of people in America as having different layers that define who they are. These layers are unpeeled to reveal our different selves depending on the circumstances. How do teachers know which micro-culture is important to an individual, family, or ethnic group other than their own? Is the macro-culture more important than the micro-cultures? Let's answer these questions by considering primary cultural domains.

Primary Cultural Domain

If I describe myself as a Southern-born, Black American, female educator who lives in Massachusetts, how many cultures do I operate within? If you guessed four, you are doing fine, based on my description. By definition, I function within several domains. And which do you imagine are my primary ones? If you heard my accent and knew me better, you might automatically guess the primary cultural domain I operate within is a traditional Southern Black culture. The way I talk, the foods I prepare, my friendliness towards everyone, my desire for hot, humid weather, and my religious background are all characteristics of this domain. But living in Boston, a Northern, cold, sometimes unfriendly environment, does not necessarily define who I am. When Roberts (1976) says that culture is "the total way of life developed and lived by a group of people, that encircles the separate and idiosyncratic meanings of persons, defining the bounds of collective understanding" (p. 1), I use her definition to refer to the way I was raised by my parents in Mississippi, in a segregated country town; my values, principles, and understanding of life were developed through the lens of my parents. Yet Roberts is also talking about my collective understanding of being female in America, as well as what it means to be female and Black in this society. How I present myself to you, and who I say I am represents a variety of cultural perspectives—some primary, some secondary, and still others even less significant. If you want to know which cultural domain is primary for someone else, educators would do well to ask that person instead of making assumptions. What are the cultural domains you function within? And which are primary for you? Make your list in the spaces provided, and place an asterisk by those you consider primary:

A. Cultural Domains

_____

_____

_____

_____

By definition each of us in the United States is multicultural, and therefore understanding cultural overlaps or connecting sub-systems is essential to our living together. **Learning where our micro-cultures or sub-systems overlap may be the first step to understanding diversity—we are different, yet we are similar.** Think about the micro-cultures you may have in common with your colleagues (common educational backgrounds, families from the same geographical areas, similar ages, similar educational philosophy, children the same ages) or those that overlap with your students, your friends.

Banks and Banks (1997) refer to multiple group memberships based on categories that define us, such as gender, race, nationality, and religion. They refer to roles we play in our lives and are another way of viewing the overlapping micro-cultures each of us incorporates in our lives. Let us deliberately think of micro-cultures or memberships of those whom we so easily marginalize, and look at the overlap with them as well. By this I mean, if you are primarily able-bodied, think of the micro-cultures you might share with someone who must use a wheel chair to get around; if you are a speaking person, think of the multiple memberships you might have with someone who is deaf; if you are part of the dominant culture, think of what you might have in common with those in the sub-dominant cultures. These type of exercises are good for children, as well as adults, and help us recognize our similarities, despite obvious differences. Take a few minutes to think about some of the micro-cultures or multiple group memberships you share with people in your environment. Write what you have in common with that group, and check the accuracy of your list with them during your next encounter.

B. Shared Micro-culture
      or group membership   **Common**
                                                      experience

_____   _____

_____   _____

_____   _____

_____   _____

Negotiating Culturally

We can learn to respect each other's cultures by learning to negotiate first within the ones we have in common. The earlier exercises should help you capitalize on what we have in common. Roberts (1976) describes how we socialize our young: "To become human, the young are socialized, taught how to behave; more importantly, they are enculturated, given a world view that, hopefully, makes sense out of the pieces of life" (p. 1). What a child learns from the adults who pass on their primary cultures is what we observe when we meet them in school. Since parents or some other responsible adults have socialized them in a particular way, it is imperative that we learn as much as we can about their cultures in order to enhance our interactions with them.

Children bring with them a variety of cultural world views that have been influenced by their families and other social institutions, such as houses of worship and neighborhood community centers. But their families do more to socialize them than any other factor. So when educators learn about the family, they understand the children better. *A different cultural world view does not mean or imply an inferior one, or a superior one, just dissimilar and probably unfamiliar.* Though there is a dominant cultural perspective operating in our country, usually referred to as ethnic European with middle-class values, dominated groups have sought to express and sustain their cultural world views in spite of their powerlessness in our society (Schaefer, 1990; Spring, 1997).

Hard lessons learned from our history of deculturalizing the Native Americans by forcing them off reservations and trying to "educate" their children through separating them from their families and removing their cultural roots, should remind us that respect for and understanding of a people's culture is essential to pave the way for communication and family involvement—two important components of helping children achieve. Most of us want this same respect for ourselves and our children (Henderson, 1986; Epstein, 1995).

To work with people who come from different cultural perspectives or world views requires a respect first for them as human beings—our most basic, common social system; then respect for their cultural world view. Respect does not necessarily connote agreement, just the recognition of their right to be who they are— a fundamental Constitutional right. The mistake we have often made in education has been the denial of others' culture and world view, and an insistence that the one held by middle-class Americans of European descent, or the dominant group, is *the* best for everyone.

The Civil Rights Movement of the 1960s, led by coalitions of White and Black Americans, came about following decades of oppression and injustice. This movement awakened many groups to seek respect for their cultures and way of life; these groups included women, the elderly, the handicapped, gay and lesbian people, as well as second language groups. It is critically important for educators to learn to respect and negotiate in others' primary cultural domains in order to teach effectively in our increasingly diverse school systems. Learning about the children's world outside of school can only aid teachers in developing a more supportive climate inside the school to facilitate learning.

There is also no need to worry about learning everything about a person's primary culture before you initiate meaningful communication with them. Of the many articles and research on teaching culturally diverse populations, the ones that focus on what happens in the classroom appeal to me the most. An article entitled "The Music Is Why I Teach: Intuitive Strategies of Successful Teachers in Culturally Diverse Classrooms" by Richard R. Powell (1996) describes an analysis of the teaching environments of four teachers from four distinct regions of the country who successfully teach children of various racial and cultural backgrounds. None of them had any formal training in diversity or multicultural education in their teacher education program and only one had participated in a diversity workshop, yet each one developed some unique ways of becoming sensitive to their diverse students so that they could improve their instructional practices in an effort to reach all the children. Powell (1996) chose the teachers because they had "demonstrated an intuitive ability to create culturally relevant instruction" and "become known in their schools for using instructional strategies that engaged all their students in learning the content" (p. 50). He discovered three common themes as he observed the teachers in their classrooms and interviewed them, their supervisors, and their building administrators:

- *Reshaping Traditional School Curriculum.* They perceived the need to reshape the prescribed curriculum they were expected to teach in order to more directly meet the cultural needs of their students . . . they clearly demonstrated a willing disposition in several key areas: they negotiated classroom curriculum with students, to put students first in their classroom decision-making; changed classroom curriculum based on implicit and explicit negotiations with students; and explored students' needs, to make those needs central to their curriculum (p. 54).

- *Rethinking the Role as Teacher: Becoming Teacher as Facilitator, Guide, and Risk-Taker.* Rethinking the curriculum necessitated this change in their roles as teacher. One teacher saw herself as mentor-friend of students; another perceived her role as a facilitator responsible for empowering students; two others actually learned Spanish, became fluent as a means of understanding their students better (one of these two began learning Chinese as her Asian population began to increase); and all were continuously learning about the backgrounds of their students, seeking ways to understand their values and to make the curriculum more relevant.

- *Acquiring and Demonstrating Cultural Sensitivity.* These teachers clearly perceived themselves to be different from their colleagues due in large part to their sensitivity to their students' backgrounds. Powell (1996) tells us that, for these teachers, "classroom decision making for teachers was based, at least in part, on students' cultural backgrounds. The instructional risks these teachers took affirmed their strong beliefs that traditional content-centered curriculum, that which represents a prescribed set knowledge and skills reflective of one cultural value system, was no longer effective for classrooms of diverse learners" (p. 56).

Are these teachers so unusual? Yes, in the sense that they have taken courageous steps to meet the needs of all their students and have discovered ways to promote success because of their students' diversity. No, in the sense that they are simply meeting the professional demands of their jobs. The demands seem greater because most of our systems are not set up to accommodate diverse student populations. **The degree to which we need to learn to negotiate in the cultures of our children and their families depends on the goals we are trying to achieve with the children, particularly with children in at-risk situations.** How does one begin to negotiate in another's culture? Is there some special way to start? What were the initial steps taken by the teachers in Powell's study? **Caring** about each student is the place to start.

Culture and Care

The work of Dr. Mel Levine offers an example of another area of human difference in which educators can negotiate across cultures. Levine makes a strong case for educators to move beyond the traditional policies and structures in schools, and focus on the needs of the child first, similar to the actions of the four teachers who focused on the needs of their children, which resulted in different decision-making strategies, as well as changes in curriculum and instructional practices.

Levine is a professor of pediatrics at the University of North Carolina School of Medicine and the Director of the Clinical Center for the Study of Development and Learning. He works regularly with educators and clinicians on learning disorders and other functional difficulties confronting children, and has been working as a physician and educator for over twenty years. His approach to working with children is unusual, and he has published widely and been recognized for his sensible approach to educating children with learning problems. In his book *Educational Care: A System for Understanding and Helping Children with Learning Problems at Home and in School* (1994), he invites educators, parents, and others working with children to focus on the child first, then move on to do whatever is necessary to ensure success for the child. He presents what he calls a phenomenological model "that favors informed observation and description over labeling and that takes into account the great heterogeneity of children with disappointing school performance. As its basis it makes use of analyses of phenomena that are known to hinder academic performance in children at different ages. This model places a strong emphasis on identifying and using the innate strengths of these children" (p. 2). What is most impressive to me is his concept of educational care, which he perceives as analogous to health care. He writes:

> Not all medical conditions require the same medicine or the same level of health care. Education too should provide a form of individualized care and, in addition, it needs to do this work with compassion . . . children arrive at school each morning with a wide range of strengths and weaknesses and therefore with diverse educational care needs. While we cannot (and should not) individualize all learning for all students, in so far as this is feasible, it is imperative to do this for those who are most in need. As with optimal health care, there should be good prevention, strong advocacy, and responsible management. (p. 6)

Levine (1994) and his colleagues believe that children with learning problems should not be isolated or stigmatized, as this only heightens their sense of feeling defective. His approach is embodied in this statement: ". . . to provide true educational care is to demonstrate authentic respect for a child's unique mind while caring about it and caring for it" (p. 278). I believe that respecting the uniqueness of a child means learning about the child and integrating that knowledge into the curriculum to ensure his or her success. Levine believes that educators and the general public must make major shifts in their thinking if they are to respect the unique needs of diverse children. He does not advocate abandoning traditional practices, but asks that we learn to make adjustments to ensure each child's educational success. It will mean gaining knowledge and understanding about the child's cultural domains, and in this case there are at least two domains to consider—the child's neurodevelopmental condition and ethnic background. He advocates shifts in a variety of traditional policies and practices to ensure success for each child. Some of these are:

- The redefinition of what we mean by normal.
- The broadening of educational requirements.
- The creation of multiple pathways toward success in children.
- The erasing of stigmas.
- Attuning schools to neurodevelopmental diversity. (pp. 272–275)

The first four points have implications for any school children, not just those with neurodevelopmental conditions, or those we often refer to as special needs. Somehow the messages of these practitioners seem to focus on giving attention to students in different ways, examining and questioning traditional methods when they don't work, instead of blaming the child or family. Levine (1994) reminds us that we practitioners must work at taking a fresh approach to old problems, and focus on success for everyone. How do we begin the process of changing our ways?

Changing is easier said than done, which is why this book is about a staff development *process*. It is very difficult to learn all you need to know about addressing the unique needs of a learner in a short span of time. Nor is it reasonable to think that one educator can or should take on a sometimes complex learning task to address the needs or concerns that others need to be aware of, including parents, the principal, and other educators on your team. Even the teachers in the next grade may need to understand the challenges you are encountering with children at risk of failing *before* the end of the school year. You may want to create a team to help you *now*.

This is called learning together—pooling your resources and getting the job done. I will discuss more details about this type of teamwork in the next chapter.

Honoring Families and Ourselves

Most families make an effort to stay connected to their primary cultural groups and expect that other adults who have responsibility for their children will respect and uphold the primary culture they have worked hard to foster. School activities and programs that work against preserving the child's culture are bound to cause conflict between families and educators, which is ultimately reflected in student performance. At the very least, educators should not denigrate the culture of any of their students, even if they choose not to celebrate or promote it. Respect and civility toward their children is the least that families can expect from educators. Understanding culture in general helps us realize how we fit into the cultural picture of our diverse country, nationally, regionally, locally, and in our schools; it facilitates expanding our understanding beyond our own cultural world view. **We are diverse and honoring diversity is honoring ourselves and others**.

How then do we build on this understanding to launch a staff development process focused on creating classrooms where **all** of our children are learning? Before turning to Chapter 3, which describes how to launch this internally driven staff development process, let us review for a few moments the barriers we face in addressing challenges encountered by educators in diverse classrooms.

Barriers to Helping All Children Achieve

1. **Limited knowledge about the history and current conditions of particular diverse groups.** Public schools, teacher education programs, in-service staff development institutes, and community programs (in public libraries, for example) all have some responsibility for teaching and sharing knowledge about the history of the people in our country. American history should at least tell us about all the people who live here and have contributed to what our country is today. Yes, this is controversial, yet we must state the truth as we know it. Call it what you choose—American History, Multicultural Education, or some other subject—knowledge about the racial and

cultural groups, history of legislation regarding schooling for girls, children with neurodevelopmental disorders and physical handicaps, bilingual education, and other groups is essential for making decisions and finding solutions to these challenges we face in schools. Without adequate understanding of history and accurate knowledge of diverse groups, it is easy for the stereotypes and misunderstandings about dominated and oppressed groups in our country to be substituted for the truth and continue to undermine success in the classrooms.

2. **Limited, outdated, fragmented or non-existent Staff Development Programs.** Reports on best practices nationally and locally remind us that *it is the quality of teaching first* that makes the biggest difference in how well children are prepared for success in school and ultimately life. Keeping abreast of the current practices of successful teachers, the research on pertinent topics, as well as the national programs that demonstrate how others meet these challenges, is vital to the success of teachers in diverse classrooms. Teachers also need planning and reflection time together; no longer is the isolation of teachers held as a symbol of best practice. Working together to critique each other's work and to support each other's learning, all of which facilitates growth for veterans and novices, is what staff developers are teaching for the present and the new century.

3. **Limited interaction with families and others who represent cultures that differ from our own.** Getting to know the families of children and interacting with them is important for teachers in accelerating the learning of children different from themselves, and different from the main or majority culture in the school. Contact with families brings about understanding that might otherwise never occur. A recent study prepared for the U. S. Department of Education, entitled *New Skills for New Schools: Preparing Teachers in Family Involvement,* proposed a framework that includes several approaches, one of which recognizes the value of cultural competence by getting to know families. The approaches include: (1) a functional approach that describes the roles and responsibilities of teachers and parents in promoting student achievement;

(2) a parent empowerment approach based on the strengths of disenfranchised families; (3) a cultural competence approach that makes the school an inclusive, respectful setting where diversity is welcomed; and (4) a social capital approach that builds community support for education (p. 20). This general framework, and the specific work of educators such as Epstein (1995) and Comer (1997) offer us options for including families and having them become more involved as partners in the education of their children—we just need to practice it more.

4. **Traditional structures, policies, and practices of public schools.** It is no secret that the majority of our schools still operate on an outdated, bureaucratic model attuned to middle-class, homogenous populations that are usually insensitive to the needs and aspiration of a diverse body of students. Traditional academic tracking policies and practices, out-dated curricula, uninspired programs for special needs children, the practice of one-dimensional pedagogy, inadequate provisions for second language learners, traditional classroom environments—all are examples of traditional structures, policies, and practices that create disadvantages for many of today's school children. Ultimately our communities are not well served or educated.

5. **Beliefs about intelligence and the capacity of all children for learning.** Despite the expanding body of research on intelligence that raises serious questions about whether intelligence is a fixed commodity, and the historical and current disagreements among psychologists on the definition of intelligence (Sternberg & Detterman, 1986), as well as the many national programs and examples of local success with children who represent groups considered to have "less intelligence," it appears that a majority of educators still believe in the fixed theory of intelligence. Even though the multiple intelligence theory of Howard Gardner, which documents the various ways children can demonstrate competence (1993), and the Vygotsky-based work of Fuerestein (1980) that demonstrates that even children disconnected from their cultures, and those with brain damage, do have the capacity to learn at high levels, traditional thinking about fixed intelligence is hard

to change. Programs such as those created by Debbie Meier (1995), Marva Collins (1991), Hank Levin (1989), and Ted Sizer (1990) demonstrate that inner-city and rural children in the worst imaginable circumstances economically, environmentally, and personally do learn to succeed, through effort and with support. Yet the negative attitude of many educators persists: *I cannot do what you do* because . . . Too many people give up too easily, because change is not easy and it is threatening. This barrier takes time to break down.

6. **Lackluster leadership in schools to promote the achievement of all children.** Principals who are instructional leaders for faculty and children are truly difficult to find in today's schools. More rare are principals and superintendents who believe in the capability of all children to learn at high levels. Thus, because of the limited vision for educating all children at the highest levels, there are few programs or strategies directed toward that end. School board members with traditional views about achievement tend to hire superintendents and principals who are also generally not concerned about all the children learning at high levels. When the policy-making bodies in a system do not advocate for all children learning at high levels, it is difficult for others in the system to become advocates for all children. It is important to assess the climate in your school and your system to determine the level of leadership you can expect in your efforts for all children. Where such leadership is absent, it is more difficult to bring about change. Strategies for managing these types of changes will be discussed in Chapter 6.

Our next step is to explore what is required to change the school environment to help all children achieve. We begin that discussion in Chapter 3, after you complete the exercises in the Diversity Notebook.

Summary Questions
Diversity and Culture

A. What strategies do I use now that are useful for all students? Distinguish these from strategies that work only with particular students?

B. How can I use the examples in the Powell article to increase my effectiveness with diverse students in my classes?

C. Caring can be demonstrated in so many ways with students. How do I communicate to students that I care about them, and their learning?

Diversity Notebook

A. Briefly describe an event, activity, or situation in which you negotiated across cultures.

B. What are the barriers you can identify that impede your progress with diverse learners? (Please add your own—my list is not exhaustive.)

C. Begin a list of activities or procedures or practices that would be affected as you consider changing the way you teach to ensure success for all children.

References

Banks, J. A., & Banks, C. A. (1997). *Multicultural education: Issues and perspectives.* Boston: Allyn and Bacon.

Collins, M. (1990). *Marva Collins' way : Returning to excellence in education.* New York: G. P. Putnams' Sons.

Collins, M., & Tamarkin, C. (1982). *Marva Collins' way.* New York: G. P. Putnam's Sons.

Comer, J. P. (1997). *Waiting for a miracle: Why schools can't solve our problems—and how we can.* New York: Penguin Putnam.

Epstein, J. L. (1995). School/family/community partnerships: Caring for the children we share. *Phi Delta Kappa 76*(5), 701–702.

Epstein, J. L. (1992). *School and family partnerships.* (Report No. 6). Baltimore: Center on Families, Communities, Schools & Children's Learning.

Fuerestein, R. (1980). *Instrumental enrichment: An intervention program for cognitive modification.* Baltimore: University Park Press.

Fullan, M. (1993). *Change forces.* New York: The Falmer Press.

Gardner, H. (1995). Reflections on multiple intelligences: Myths and messages. *Phi Delta Kappa 77*(3), 202–209.

Gardner, H. (1993). *Multiple intelligences: The theory in practice.* New York: Basic Books.

Goodlad, J. (1996). *Democracy, education and community.* In R. Soder, (Ed.), *Democracy, education and the schools* (p. 112). San Francisco: Jossey-Bass.

Henderson, A. T., & Berla, N. (Eds.) (1995). *A new generation of evidence: The family is critical to student achievement.* Washington, DC: Center for Law and Education.

Henderson, A. T., Marburger, C. L. & Oooms, T. (1986). *Beyond the bake sale: An educator's guide to working with parents.* Columbia, MD: National Committee for Citizens in Education.

Levin, H., Hopfenberg, W. S. & Associates (1993). *The accelerated schools: Resource guide.* San Francisco: Jossey-Bass.

Levine, M. (1994). *Educational care: A system for understanding and helping children with learning problems—at home and in school.* Cambridge, MA: Edcuators Publishing Service, Inc.

Meier, D. (1995). *The power of their ideas.* Boston: Beacon Press.

Powell, R. (1996). The music is why I teach: Intuitive strategies of successful teachers in culturally diverse learning environments. *Teaching & Teacher Education,* 12 (1), 49–61

Roberts, J. I. (1976). Cultural patterns of education. In J. I. Roberts & S. K. Akinsanya (Eds.), *Schooling in the cultural context* (pp. 1–21). New York: David McKay Company.

Schaefer, R. T. (1990). *Racial and ethnic groups.* New York: HarperCollins.

Shartrand, A. M., Weiss, H. B., Kreider, H. M., & Lopez, M. E. (1997). *New skills for new schools: Preparing teachers in family involvement.* Washington, DC: U. S. Department of Education.

Sizer, T. R. (1992). *Horace's compromise.* Boston: Houghton Mifflin.

Sizer, T. R. (1992). *Horace's school: Redesigning the American high school.* Boston: Houghton Mifflin.

Spring, J. (1997). *Deculturalization and the struggle for equality: A brief history of the education of dominated cultures in the United States.* New York: McGraw-Hill.

Sternberg, R. J., & Detterman, D. K. (Eds.) (1986). *What is intelligence? Contemporary viewpoints on its nature and definition.* Norwood, NJ: Ablex.

Vygotsky, L. S. (1978). *Mind in society: The development of higher psychological processes.* Cambridge: Harvard University Press.

Wolcott, H. (1976). Culture, community and school. In J. I. Roberts & S. K. Akinsanya (Eds.), *Schooling in the cultural context* (pp. 23–44). New York: David McKay Company.

CHAPTER 3

Beliefs, Pedagogy, and Change

In this chapter I will describe the approach I am recommending that you use to move toward greater cultural competence. We have a professional and moral responsibility to exhaust our resources to meet the educational needs of each child, instead of deferring to the traditions of the system or to our own sense of powerlessness to make significant change in our classrooms or systems. Your own sense of efficacy is very important in this task. Learning successful change strategies can strengthen your sense of efficacy and expand your repertoire of pedagogical tools to help each child achieve at high levels.

The Change Process

Change is threatening to many people, and if the importance and relevance of it for their lives is not clear, few will attempt to do it. After all, change usually means that you will have to do something different, alter your routines, which means experiencing some discomfort, at least initially. The first change may be in the way we think about what we need to do as individuals. So changing ourselves is the first order of business. *Am I really interested in making a commitment to educate all the children well? This probably means more work for me; and I feel that I am already at my limit with school-related work. Why must I be the one to change?* If these kinds of thoughts run through your mind, then you can be sure that you are having a normal reaction to yet another idea or set of ideas for teachers to try out in the classroom.

Any one who thinks about how change happens knows that it is a *very personal* issue; how each of us responds to change determines whether there is any change. Before I offer you a bit of history about staff development and present a tool for managing the change process, it will be helpful if you consider these general ideas about the change process.

- You must consider what the meaning of change is, what the impact will be on your life; this can never be underestimated because change is **personal**.

- Yet, working with a team is the most effective way to manage major reform, with each person having a specific role to play.

- This necessarily means collaboration, building trust and relationships for supporting and learning from each other.

- Change is a developmental process and *always* takes more time than you plan for it.

- There are identifiable stages of the process, but it is not linear and can be frustrating if you expect it to be straightforward and sequential.

- Chaos is normal in the beginning, otherwise you are not making significant changes; this will lessen as the process evolves if it is managed properly.

- Effective communication and monitoring of the process is essential for making progress.

- Short-term and long-term rewards are necessary to keep people motivated.

- The process is both a top-down and bottom-up enterprise; both central administration and the school must be involved in appropriate ways—as a system each must at least keep the other informed and avoid working independently.

Lack of adequate support for implementation has doomed many a reform. Careful attention to provide technical and instructional support are critical for at least one year after a major change has taken place (Crandall, 1989; Fullan, 1993).

Despite its unpredictable nature, the change process can be as enriching for educators as it is for the student who benefit from the change (Berman & McLaughlin, 1978; Fullan, 1991, 1993; Loucks-Horsley & Stiegelbauer, 1991). These ideas should whet your appetite about what you can expect when you begin the process of change. They are thoughts to keep in mind as you envision how you and your colleagues can initiate the needed reform in your schools.

The Change Process and Staff Development

Educational literature is replete with studies on the need for school reform and how it can happen. Innovations for school improvement focused on primarily administrative issues in the 1970s, but did not necessarily focus on the teaching and learning process (Loucks-Horsely & Hall, 1997). Those days of passive staff development (when administrators decided what teachers needed, usually without their input) are indeed passé in many places (Sparks & Hirsh, 1997), due in part to greater teacher participation in their own development, new legislation about certification, public demand for more accountability from schools, and national standards.

An innovative approach to address change in the teaching and learning process was offered by Loucks-Horsley and Hall (1978) when they introduced the now popular and effective Concerns-Based Adoption Model (C-BAM), which resulted from research in school and college settings. In their book, *Change in Schools, Facilitating the Process*, Hall and Hord (1987) describe their research in detail, showing the three dimensions of the C-BAM model, including the stages of concern, levels of use, and innovation configuration. The stage of concerns dimension became very popular, because it was such a common reflection of educators' experience. These educational researchers report that the C-BAM was not designed as a model process for change, but as a *tool* to facilitate change: "The C-BAM does not prescribe a specific set of strategies for change, rather it provides useful information for those whose role it is to help teachers change their curriculum and instructional approaches" (1987, p. 17).

The six stages of the C-BAM model range from an Awareness level, where a person has little to no concern about an innovation, to Refocusing, the stage of implementation and use where people begin to find new or alternative ways to adapt the innovation. The attraction in the model is that it reflects basic human responses to a new idea presented by someone else, and focuses on the immediate concerns of teachers as they contemplate change. The first three stages (Awareness, Informational, and Personal) mirror a process of hearing, collecting data, and trying to see how this relates to the individual.

The next three (Management, Consequence, and Collaboration) respectively address early use of the innovation, the impact and relevance it has on teaching and students, and how the innovation can fit with others in the school. Refocusing, the final stage, finds the teacher engaged in thinking about how to improve the innovation. The authors have presented the behavioral responses to the stages of concern when considering a new idea in this chart:

Stages of Concern	Expressions of Concern
6. Refocusing	I have some ideas about something that would work even better.
5. Collaboration	How can I relate what I am doing to what others are doing?
4. Consequence	How is my use affecting kids? How can I refine it to have more impact?
3. Management	I seem to be spending all my time getting materials ready.
2. Personal	How will using it affect me?
1. Informational	I would like to know more about it.
0. Awareness	I am not concerned about it. (Adapted from Hord, Rutherford, Huling-Austin & Hall, 1987)

This dimension of the model and the work of other researchers has added to the knowledge about managing change. Research and practice both indicate that change is a very personal issue, therefore addressing how it will affect people and their lives must be a priority, especially when major change or reform is being considered. Ignoring how *personal change is* simply stalls the process until folks can find meaning for themselves and become more settled about how the change will impact them (Fullan, 1993; Loucks-Horsley & Stiegelbauer, 1991). The social concerns dimension of the C-BAM model appears to be a model that embraces the personal issues and paves the way for the process to evolve.

Change can be managed effectively and accelerated if leadership is in place with a clear understanding about the complexity of the change process. The challenge of change is to prepare people to be ready for it on an on-going basis. Fullan (1993) announces in his most user-friendly book to date, *Change Forces,* that "it is no longer acceptable to separate planned change from seemingly spontaneous or naturally occurring change. It is only by raising our consciousness and insights about the *totality* of educational change that we can do something about it. We learn that it is not possible to solve 'the change problem,' but we can learn to live with it more proactively and more productively" (p. vii).

This is welcome news for those of us who recognize that we have to commit to the process for change, ideally with a strong supportive team, to meet the demands of professional development for ourselves and our students. And when the cost of not changing is wasted lives, few educators can deliberately sit back and ignore what is happening. So how do we set the stage for change? Schools are an integral part of our larger society, therefore, what happens in society will definitely be reflected in schools. So as change happens around us, we must be better prepared to handle those changes that influence our lives inside schools.

National Models

School change is happening, but not on a scale that meets the growing needs of our students. Despite successful programs developed for many years by educators such as Deborah Meier of Central

Park East, Marva Collins of Westside Preparatory, James Comer of the Professional Development Program, and Hank Levin's Accelerated Schools Program, to list some of the more prominent ones, thousands of urban, suburban, and rural schools still have major problems educating the majority of their children. This is especially true for children who are poor, disabled, English language learners, or children who simply have other distinguishing characteristics, such as being female, that evoke differential educational treatment in schools. Educators across the country are still groping for answers; many continue to blame the children and their families for these failures; others ignore the lessons of successful programs; and most frightening of all, *many are convinced of their inability to make a difference in the lives of these children and their schools.*

Yet many conscientious educators, especially teachers, are already responding proactively to the challenge of educating all the children, just as you learned from the Powell and Levine references above. It is not easy to make major changes in schools (not just the classrooms) while meeting the everyday responsibilities of the teaching and learning process. This challenge to change can be exacting and requires serious preparation to create: (1) a vision about what you want schools to become, (2) collaborative sessions with peers internally, and with external groups, and (3) supportive administration at all levels. What may not be so obvious is that when you begin to consider a goal as large and as magnanimous as educating all the children at high levels, you are speaking about transforming not just classrooms, but schools and communities. It begins with you thinking differently about your goal as an educator, collaborating with others who commit to the goal, and using the process to get things moving—one step at a time.

A Conscious, Reflective Change Strategy

It is important for staff development not to happen in a vacuum, but to exist as part of a process that can be rewarding to the individual, the school, and the profession. Each of us must also be as vigilant as possible to stay abreast of the changes in our society that affect us personally and professionally. Thus, if we are to manage our responses to differences in children, then the most effective way to manage this diversity is by utilizing a conscientious process attuned to the changing world, undergirded by current knowledge in professional areas that addresses the needs of our children and our respective disciplines. Beyond being aware of how you respond to change, here are four lenses through which to view the process of first changing yourselves, and then your classrooms and schools:

1. Examining your beliefs and knowledge about diverse groups. It is important that you become aware and conscious of your own beliefs, experiences, and feelings related to the human differences you encounter from day-to-day. This will enable you to separate our own prejudices and biases from the immediate circumstances, thus facilitating a more fair and just outcome for students. What you believe has a powerful effect on how you behave, therefore it is vitally important that you understand what you believe.

Carr (1979) tells us that belief is confidence in an alleged fact without positive proof. It is easy from this definition to see how one might get in trouble by simply acting on one's beliefs! Rokeach (1973), who has done extensive research on belief systems, tells us that every person has a belief system. And that the strengths of our beliefs about any particular idea depends on how central they are to our belief system. Rokeach defines beliefs this way: "[Belief]. .. transcends attitudes toward objects and situations; is a standard that guides and determines action, attitudes toward objects and situations, ideology, presentations of self to others, evaluations, judgments, justifications, comparisons of self with others and attempts to influence others" (p. 25). His research has revealed that the stronger one holds a belief, the more resistant it is to change. *This implies that we weight the strength of our beliefs about different things.* Again, this is a signal for us to make an effort to understand even how we come to feel so strongly about what we believe.

Ask yourself what you believe about a particular group of people different from yourself. How strong are your beliefs about this group? Now think about the human diversity in your classroom. What beliefs do you have about children of different racial groups? About those with different physical capabilities? Can you gauge the strength of your beliefs about these students? More important, can you gauge the strength of your belief about their capacity to learn in your classroom? ***Examining and understanding your response to these questions can only help you in preparing to work with children from diverse backgrounds who are at risk of educational failure.*** *Think about the question and your answers, then discuss them with a trusted colleague. This type of self-reflection with a trusted colleague is vitally important to your working effectively with diverse students.*

A safe environment is essential when examining your beliefs, because it is important for people to feel at ease to share what they believe and to ask *any* type of question so learning about each other can occur. Understanding, for example, your personal histories and experience about people of other races makes you conscious of the different responses you have to people of different races. Acknowledging your biases and stereotypes also allows you to study and discuss the societal racism and the discriminating behaviors that exist. Not acknowledging your own feelings, prejudices, stereotypes, and misunderstandings about race handicaps you when it comes to working honestly and authentically with students and peers who are aware (at various levels of understanding, depending on age, life experience, etc.) of the societal and institutional racism and discrimination that are real in their everyday lives. Remaining ignorant about obvious societal problems such as racism, discrimination against people with disabilities, homophobia, and sexism also denies the reality of life in America, but particularly denies the reality of those in our country who are treated as second-class citizens.

Dr. Beverly Daniels Tatum, a psychologist and authority on the psychology of racism, adopts Wellman's (1977) definition of racism as "a system of advantage based on race" (1992, p. 3) in her article on racial identity development theory, which evolved from her classes on racism at Holyoke College and her own research on the topic. Her work is a valuable resource in helping adults recognize their own stage of development concerning racial issues, as well as other inequities in our society that can go unnoticed by people who have not experienced them on a regular basis.

Our perceptions about others can be based on facts, fantasies, hearsay, TV news or commercials, and certainly can be influenced by our families' beliefs. We are responsible for our behavior and how we respond in our school settings. Therefore, it is imperative that we consciously and deliberately behave in responsible, respectable ways in our profession. Acknowledgment and recognition of our beliefs and knowledge about diverse groups make our experiences easier to discuss and examine. Having these experiences makes us more comfortable and competent, to respond to queries and circumstances that arise in our classrooms with children, their families, and our professional colleagues. Working through these beliefs and experiences can be frustrating and liberating at the same time.

Stop for a few minutes and think about how Tatum's definition of racism could be adapted to represent the other types of diversity in schools.

- What would you call a system of advantage based on physical abilities? _____.

- What would you call a system of advantage based on gender? _____.

- What would you call a system of advantage based on geographic location? _____.

- Can you think of other systems of advantage in our society that exclude one or more groups? The whole picture of discrimination and racial, gender, or able-bodied prejudice is not as useful in your journey toward cultural competence if you view the problem as isolated to one group or another. Ideally you must view the systems of advantage in a democratic society as wrong and immoral.

Understanding your students, their histories, cultures, and ways of life will enable you to teach them more effectively. Your beliefs about and understanding affects how you treat students, just as your beliefs, knowledge, and understanding of those in your own cultural group influences how you feel about them and how you treat them. Knowing only the history and culture of some of your students places you at a disadvantage, while having the advantage of knowing others more fully. This imbalance ultimately robs you and your students of rich histories, interactions, and opportunities to learn from each other.

Here are a few short questions to get you thinking about your beliefs and knowledge about diverse populations in our country.

1. Was segregation ever legal or constitutional in the United States?

2. Can you identify the children who were separated from their families to be educated outside the community or neighborhood schools?

3. Using a scale of 1 to 10, with 10 the highest score, can you rate the climate of race relations (among ethnic groups present) during these periods in the U.S.: 1850 1900 1950 1998? Who is responsible for improving race relations in the U. S.?

4. Does our Constitution protect the right to a public education for women, people with disabilities, and people with a different sexual orientation?

5. Do people who are not yet citizens (legal residents, for example) deserve the same access to public schools as citizens?

Answer these questions on your own; then ask family, friends, or colleagues who are of another race or ethnic group, or of a different human condition than you, to answer them. Begin the discussions with each other, find the facts, and discover how much you know and how much you have to learn to become more conversant and familiar with these topics. Later, when you are planning for your classes, or for improving the climate in your school for all children, you will have a different perspective and new knowledge-base from which to work.

2. Becoming more reflective about professional behavior and pedagogy. This requires developing a means of examining and analyzing your instructional behavior generally, especially when working with children from diverse backgrounds. Your motivation and goals need to be examined, as with any professional action, to determine whether your pedagogical practices are in substance and spirit representative of your role as educators. Donald Schon (1983) introduces an important process to many professions with his work on reflection-in-action and reflection-on-action, which require professionals to develop habits for continuous learning and problem solving by consciously thinking about complex problems.

Becoming more reflective will not only assist you in being more conscientious about all your work, but will also help you discern whether your feelings or thoughts are within you, with the behavior of the child, or simply in the social circumstances in which they occur.

My thoughts about reflections on professional behavior are quite simple. Professional people need to be accountable to themselves as well as to others; and you can only benefit through consciously thinking in the moment or re-thinking about what you say and do. As a teacher of teachers, I have learned the value of giving myself feedback, and asking for it from others. In class I want to be clear about why I do things and I want students to understand why, as well. I am also convinced that being reflective is one of the more productive ways to improve quickly and to keep learning. For me, it is a way of being mindful, present-in-the-moment, and ultimately clear about what I do. Children and young people can be counted on to ask adults the "why questions"; as educators we certainly should strive to answer them. Answering "why questions" for ourselves, however, is an important step in our own understanding.

General Reflections on Professional Behavior. Reflection is thinking back, critiquing what happened, remembering your behavior and thoughts and learning from them. Since I believe reflection is important for teachers, I build reflective activities into all my courses. Through keeping a journal, students can reflect on readings and class discussions; in class we analyze case studies and do problem-solving together. Other times students are asked to write short position papers on specific topics and share their perspectives on current educational events. I highly recommend these individual and group reflective practices when planning strategies to support all children learning. Another personal benefit of reflection is the time you have "to hear yourself think." (While raising us, my mother often requested that the six of us lower our voices so she could hear herself think!) "Hearing yourself think" is another way to examine ideas before or after you express them.

The individual activities I require of students are similar to Schon's (1983) reflection-**on**-action, which he describes as happening for teachers before and after a lesson—deliberate, planned thinking and preparation for teaching. He then relates how teachers answer questions or react to problems unexpectedly, for example, during class, Schon calls this reflection-**in**-action. His work focuses almost entirely on the individual as reflector and reminds us of the importance of this activity for our own growth. There are, however, other important benefits of reflecting with others.

The collaborative team effort referred to by some change advocates is meant to move teachers forward, individually and collectively, to a higher state of the art in the pedagogy. These interactions are thought of as regular opportunities to reflect in a variety of ways. For example, planning, problem solving, and making curricula decisions are all enhanced through collaboration. These meaningful discourses are anchored in the mission or current goals of programs that are connected to the school mission. Thus, this definition of professional development by Darling-Hammond & McLaughlin (1995) stresses the interactive and progressive role they envision for teachers: "Professional development . . . prepares teachers to see complex subject matter from the perspective of diverse students . . . and today also means providing occasions for teachers to reflect critically on their practice and fashion new knowledge and beliefs about content, pedagogy, and learners" (p. 597). The emphasis and importance of reflection is meant to reduce the isolation that is so common to the teaching profession, and to emphasize the interactive nature of learning for teachers, as well as students. Here are a couple of suggestions to stimulate your thinking about the benefits of making time to be more reflective about your work:

1. Recall the last time you wished you had more time to work through a problem with a lesson, or a response to a parent or colleague. Usually these are times when you were rushed, feeling strong emotions about an issue, or when you were not paying close attention to the situation at hand.

2. Now, recall another situation in which you wanted to consult with others about a complex problem, but you felt pressured to make a decision before it was possible to do so. So you didn't consult anyone. Sometimes we ignore those inner messages that tell us to *spend more time on this one.*

Consider how different the outcomes might have been had you thought more about the situations, or had you invited others to help you with problem solving, or just to help you see the situation from another perspective. When you have a vision or dream of how educational practices might be, and you have set annual goals to work toward realizing the vision, then it makes sense that you develop some measures to determine how you are progressing. Reflecting alone or with others can be a critical aspect of analyzing progress toward your vision. More often than not, however, your pedagogical practices are a key determinant of your success. These practices must be appropriate, otherwise learning for all simply does not occur. Begin to think of ways to build reflective time into your day.

Reflections on Pedagogical Practices. Recent national reports from commissions and task forces, and comparisons of the academic achievement of America with that of other countries around the world, imply that American children are not learning as much or as well as children from some underdeveloped nations, and that American children are performing significantly worse than children in the industrial nations considered our peers (Holmes Report, 1995; What Matters Most: Teaching for America's Future, 1996; Third International Mathematics and Science Study, 1998). How we teach—primarily a teacher-centered process—and who we teach—a diversified, heterogeneous population (versus the homogeneity of some countries such as Japan)—are often offered as the reasons for America's poor performance. Both responses warrant further investigation, since children at risk of educational failure are particularly vulnerable to being used as scapegoats by some educators who hear these responses. Research in this area suggests that when teachers act as facilitators and children are active participants, learning increases. Fewer lectures, more hands-on problem solving, and integrating technology in the curricula are just a few examples of teaching that is more children-centered. Let's move on now to take a look at the third lens of this framework, which incorporates some aspects of the first two.

3. Understanding the change process. Being aware and actively conscious of your own beliefs, experiences, and responses to change is critical to responding effectively to the needs of diverse school populations. Michael Fullan (1993), a prominent scholar who studies the change process, tells us in his book *Change Forces* that reforms and change in schools simply cannot happen successfully or in sustained ways without teacher involvement. He emphatically states that "Teachers as change agents is the *sine qua non* of getting anywhere" (p. 6). He further argues that ". . . the problem of productive change simply cannot be addressed unless we treat continuous teacher education—pre-service and in-service—as the major vehicle for producing teachers as moral change agents" (p. 7). A major question then is "How can we get teachers more involved in meaningful ways?" Fullan's answer is that teachers need to view themselves as change agents. He defines change agency as "being self-conscious about the nature of change and the change process" (p. 12). This is another level of awareness, which complements the ideas of being aware of what you believe (first lens) and taking time to be reflective (second lens) about what you say and do—but is centered on the process of change, the third lens of the framework.

Research on successful school reform or major change in schools reveal that it requires several years, usually a minimum of three, and that teachers and their instructional practices should be at the core of it (Fullan & Hargreaves, 1992; Goodlad, 1990; Sarason, 1993). Conversely, the failure of school reform often is attributable to the lack of change in the basic structure, policies, and instructional practices of the school or system, because teachers are not involved in the process. In many school systems, teachers are on the periphery of change and are seen in very traditional ways—as having command of their isolated classrooms, but not as leaders in schools. However, both practice and research indicate that when seeking a different outcome for student performance, or a higher level of achievement, involving teachers in the process is crucial to the endeavor (Boyer, 1995; Fullan, 1993; Sarason, 1996; Darling-Hammond, 1995).

The more we understand the way change happens, the more we can anticipate the journey, which enables us to better manage our responses to it. Knowing ourselves in this way helps us separate our personal reaction to addressing diversity from our reaction to the process of change itself. Being sensitive to what is happening in the world around us and how events affect us personally and at school is very important in understanding our response to change. How do you begin to assess how to become involved in the change process? Fullan (1993) offers four core capacities for building the process to manage change: personal vision building, inquiry, mastery, and collaboration. Though in some ways the terms are self-explanatory, I will offer brief explanations to ensure that their meaning is clear.

- *Personal vision building.* Your personal dream of what you can do in the profession is the basis of personal vision building. This review forces study of your strengths and weaknesses, as well as a look at the goals for the children and families you influence. Aspiring to attain your personal vision keeps you motivated to pursue it vigorously, despite the obstacles—because you believe in it. Your personal vision is the key to your own development in the profession, as well as the development of the children, families, and other lives you influence.

- *Inquiry.* This means internalizing norms, habits, and techniques for continuous learning. It also means pushing yourself and testing the quality of your work through reflective practices. These practices might include journalizing, peer mentoring and coaching or videotaping sessions to critique your methods.

- *Mastery.* Teachers are expected to be competent in their fields of study, and to be continuous learners through professional development activities. Active participation in professional activities, such as action research, collaborating with peers, and professional reading and membership in professional organizations, ensures continuous learning for educators. Mastery builds the confidence that professionals need, especially when facing new challenges; it's the one known factor you can count on in tackling new situations. "Personal mastery teaches us not to lower our vision, even if it seems as if the vision is impossible" (Senge et al., 1994, p. 195).

- *Collaboration.* Working together to bring about a synergy that could not happen without a group belies the comfort of working alone. Learning from others' perspectives, developing trust as a team, finding assistance with a troubling challenge, and becoming empowered through your collective strengths can only happen if you are working together, building a team (Fullan, 1993, pp. 12–17).

4. Building a network of resources. The fourth and final lens of the change strategy focuses on building relationships with individuals and groups who have a stake in providing effective educational experiences for all children. Such a network begins with families, and then spreads to the larger institutions and organizations in the communities. Even though traditionally the parents of school-age children have demonstrated the greatest involvement in schools, every citizen, especially tax-paying citizens, should have a vested interest in schools. What happens or does not happen in them affects us all.

Networking with families. "The influence of the home on children's success at school is profound. Whether indirectly, as models, or directly, as readers or homework helpers, parents' learning-related and school-related activities at home have a very strong influence on children's long-term academic success" (Zeigler, 1987, p. 5). Zeigler's findings have been reported in many studies with different school-age children, whose parents have different incomes and whose homes are in different communities. The research findings are clear—family involvement not only makes a difference in academic outcomes for children, but many studies show that school involvement empowers parents to learn and become citizen participants in other situations as well.

No matter what the research indicates or what other people's experiences are, you will not develop those positive, caring relationships with families if you are not committed to doing so, and open to learning about them. Excuses can be given for your lack of involvement with families, and blame apportioned to parents and families after one or two attempts to get the parents to come to school. The truth is that it's hard work to involve some parents, but calling a meeting at an inconvenient, inappropriate time and then blaming them for not showing up is tantamount to expecting interest on a savings account without depositing the money. First you have to get to know the parents. You have to make an investment first before you can expect a dividend. Too many educators never make contact with the families or people who know the communities before arranging that traditional meeting at school—which is the same way it was done 25 years ago.

Family structures and home support are different now that both parents are working, making the time after the school day a challenge for parents. For example, over half our children come from divorced households. Just this fact alone changes the dynamics of an educator's relationship with children and families. It is no longer certain who is called if there is an emergency, who attends conferences and back-to-school night, who signs report cards and permission slips, and it goes on. What the volumes of research done over the last several decades will tell you, and what is still true about parents, is that the overwhelming majority are concerned about their children's education. The volumes by Henderson & Berla (1995), which summarize the major research about families and schools, tell us that most families are very interested in their children's education, regardless of income, ethnicity, or geographic area. The research also indicates that many families do not know how to help their children and want more effective communication from educators to help them.

Joyce Epstein (1992) and her colleagues have been working with educators and families for over twenty years to discover the best ways to work together to enhance children's learning. This six-part typology is based on the theory that families and school and communities **share** responsibility for children's learning. Her framework of six types of family involvement include: (1) *the basic family parenting* responsibilities that create a supportive home environment for the child; (2) *effective communication* designed by family members and educators to facilitate sharing of information about school and the child's progress; (3) *volunteering* in a variety of ways beneficial to schools and family members learning how to help; (4) *learning at home* refers to ways children can be helped with homework by parents, who learn how to help from educators; (5) *decision making* activities that provide families with opportunities to have a voice as leaders in school business, on school councils, the PTA, or working on the budget; and (6) *collaboration with the community* to assist in developing and integrating resources to support school programs, such as developing relationships with artistic groups to expand the humanities curriculum in the school.

The work of Epstein (1992) and her colleagues at The Center on Families, Community Schools and Children's Learning is based on the theory of the overlapping interacting influences of family, school and community, with the child at the center and as the focus of everyone's energy and interest. Some schools and families and community people see themselves operating separately with well defined, segregated roles—and as a result children's learning suffers. Working together, building trust and respect for each other's primary roles, learning about each other's unique and common traits, and sharing and working together to benefit the child is a model that represents the same type of relationship described earlier when discussing teachers. It is the same kind of joint action and relationship building that occurs when people work together for the same goal.

Here are a few final recommendations about involving families: (1) do whatever is necessary to build the type of relationships that foster parents learning from each other and teaching each other about school and community issues; (2) evaluate everything you do with families, so you can keep doing what works, and drop the rest; (3) share your development and new skills working with families with your colleagues through workshops, newsletters, or other types of presentations—to the school committee, for example; and (4) monitor your progress by reviewing your goals periodically, analyzing your progress, and resetting your goals if necessary.

Using the Framework

These four areas—examining our beliefs and knowledge about diverse groups, becoming more reflective about our professional behavior, understanding the change process, and building a network of resources—represent the guide or framework for understanding this staff development resource. I believe that these four phenomena play very important roles in helping or hindering problem solving when working with diverse populations. Though I gave them to you in a particular order, when you are responding to problems, all of them can be utilized in varying degrees to move you toward your goals. For example, the first two lenses—examining your beliefs and knowledge about diverse groups and becoming more reflective about your behavior—are both necessary when you are defining or analyzing a problem or situation. The third and fourth lenses—understanding the change process and building a network of resources—are needed more when you are deciding on a plan of action.

Before this chapter, I spent two chapters presenting the definition of diversity, discussing culture, and providing some background for you to understand the challenges we face in educating the diverse students we have in our schools, as well as the difficulty we find ourselves in with so many at risk of failing in schools. I offer this framework for you to use with the rest of the book as I present the heart of the challenge we face—helping diverse children achieve at high levels. I am convinced that using this framework can influence powerful changes for you and your children. You will begin to use the framework in Chapter 4.

Summary Questions
Beliefs, Pedagogy, and Change

A. What recent change in school or my classroom can I analyze to discern the way I respond to the change process?

B. Which of my trusted colleagues can I ask to support me in examining my beliefs about groups different from myself?

C. What are some initial steps I can take to develop more reflective practices about my teaching?

D. Which individuals or groups in the community are equipped to contribute to the educational plan for a particular child?

Diversity Notebook

Here is an exercise and a few more questions to help you begin to raise your consciousness a little higher about your belief and knowledge about people different from yourself. These can be done individually, or with others whom you trust and feel will give you honest feedback, without judging you.

A.   **Stereotypes**. Stereotyping comes naturally, once we learn a few things about others, have heard a few more things, and perhaps have had some interactions with the group. Most of us have heard of stereotypes concerning most groups, even if we have never met a person representing that group. A working definition of stereotypes is that they are unreliable generalizations made about a group of people without regard to individual differences within the group (Schaefer, 1990). Try this exercise. It can generate all kinds of emotions, so it is important to remember that it is a consciousness-raising exercise to assist us in understanding our own responses to people different from ourselves. Take it seriously, but have fun.

List the names of various ethnic and racial groups in our society at the top of a column on a sheet of paper. Examples are Puerto Ricans, Italians, Native Americans, Asians, African Americans, Whites, Jews. Add people who are viewed as having some disadvantage in our society, such as Women, Homosexuals, Old People, the Handicapped; once you get started, it will be easy to shift to groups more representative of your school or community.

- Think about the meaning of stereotypes, and the impact they can have on individuals. Does knowing them influence people's behavior? How?
- List all the stereotypes you have heard about each group. (It is not important whether you believe the stereotype.)
- Compare the list, and find any similarities.
- Think about ways that stereotypes are hurtful. Give examples.
- Are stereotypes based on facts? Explain, please.
- Think about how old children are when stereotypes begin to get into their heads. How might stereotypes influence the thinking and behavior of the person being stereotyped? How might stereotypes influence the thinking and behavior of the individual doing the stereotyping?

Now, describe your feelings during the exercise. Were you nervous? Did you have fun? Did you learn any new stereotypes? You can learn to know your comfort level with different groups this way, or just become more conscious of how you discuss these issues. Finally, describe the relationship between stereotypes and beliefs about a group.

B. Think about what you normally do when someone communicates a stereotype to you about another group. Are you satisfied with your behavior? If not, what could you do to become more satisfied with a future response? How would you like your students to respond to such a situation?

C. What can you do—in your school, in your classroom—to help staff and students become aware of their stereotypes? Examine how stereotypes might influence their thinking and behavior, then consider ways to change thinking and behavior.

References

Apple, M. W., & Beane, J. A. (1995). *Democratic schools*. Alexandria, VA: Association for Supervision and Curriculum Development.

Bernian, P., & McLaughlin, M. W. (1978). *Federal programs supporting educational change: Volume 8. Implementing and sustaining innovations*. Santa Monica: Raud Corporation (R-1589-HEW/8).

Boyer, E. (1995). *The basic school: A community for learning*. Princeton, NJ: The Carnegie Foundation for the Advancement of Teaching.

Carr, J. (1979). *Communicating and relating*. Menlo Park, CA: Benjamin/Cummings Publishing.

Darling-Hammond, L., & McLaughlin, M. (1995). Policies that support professional development in an era of reform. *Phi Delta Kappa, 76* (8), 597–604.

Dewey, J. (1916). *Democracy and education*. New York: Macmillan.

Epstein, J. L. (1992). *School and family partnerships*. (Report No. 6). Baltimore: Center on Families, Communities, Schools & Children's Learning.

Ford, D. Y. (1992). Determinants of underachievement as perceived by gifted, above average, and average Black students. *Roeper Review, 14* (3), 130–136.

Ford, D. Y., & Harris III, J. (1994). Reform and gifted Black students: Promises and practices in Kentucky. *Journal for the Education of the Gifted, 17*(3), 216–240.

Fullan, M. (1991). *The new meaning of educational change*. New York: Teachers College Press.

Fullan, M. (1993). *Change forces*. New York: The Falmer Press.

Fullan M., & Hargreaves, A. (Eds.) (1992). *Teacher development and educational change.* Washington, DC: The Falmer Press.

Goodlad, J. I., Soder, R., & Sirotnik, K. A. (Eds.) (1990). *Places where teachers are taught.* San Francisco: Jossey-Bass.

Hall, G. E., & Hord, S. M. (1987). *Change in Schools, Facilitating the process.* Albany, NY: State University of New York Press.

Henderson, A. T., & Berla, N. (1995). *A new generation of evidence: The family is critical to student achievement.* Washington, DC: Center for Law and Education.

Howard, J. (1990). *Efficacy Institute Training Manual.* Lexington, MA: The Efficacy Institute.

Katzenmeyer, M., & Moller, G. (1996). The promise of teacher leadership. In R. Ackerman (Ed.), *Every teacher as a leader: Realizing the potential of teacher leadership.* San Francisco: Jossey-Bass.

Loucks-Harsley, S. & Stiegelbauer, S. (1997). Using knowledge of change to guide staff development. In H. Lieberman and L. Miller (Eds.), *Staff development for education in the '90s* (pp. 15–36). New York: Teachers College Press.

Meier, D. (1995). *The power of their ideas.* Boston: Beacon Press.

Office of Educational Research and Improvement (OERI) Urban Superintendent's Network. (1987). *Dealing with dropouts: The urban superintendent's call to action.* Washington, DC: Department of Education.

Report of the National Commission on Teaching and America's Future. (1996). *What matters most: Teaching for America's future.* New York: Teachers College.

Rokeach, M. (1968). *Beliefs, attitudes, and values.* San Francisco: Jossey-Bass.

Sadker, M., & Sadker, D. (1994). *Failing at fairness: How America's schools cheat girls.* New York: Scribner's.

Sarason, S. B. (1993). *The case for change.* San Francisco: Jossey-Bass,

Schaefer, R. T. (1990). *Racial and ethnic groups.* New York: HarperCollins.

Schon, D. A. (1983). *The reflective practitioner.* New York: HarperCollins.

Senge, P., Kleiner, A., Roberts, C., Ross, R., & Smith, B. (1994). *The fifth discipline fieldbook: Strategies and tools for building a learning organization.* New York: Bantam Doubleday Dell Publishing Group.

Sparks, D., & Hirsh, S. (1997). *A new version for staff development.* Alexandria, VA: Association for Supervision and Curriculum Development.

Tatum, B. D. (1992). Talking about race, learning abut racism. An application of racial identity theory in the classroom. *Harvard Educational Review 62* (1), 1–24.

The Holmes Group (1986). *Tomorrow's teachers.* East Lansing, MI: Author.

Willman, D. (1977). *Portraits of white racism.* Cambridge: Cambridge University Press.

Zeigler, S. (1987). The effects of parent involvement on children's achievement: The significance of home/school links. In A. T. Henderson & N. Berla (Eds.), *A new generation of evidence: The family is critical to student achievement* (pp. 151, 152). Washington, DC: Center for Law and Education.

CHAPTER 4

Diversity and Achievement

Assessing Intelligence

Since we have had some discussion about beliefs, I want to move you into the heart of the discussion about whether all children can achieve. Answering the question "Can all children achieve?" is directly related to your beliefs about a child's intelligence. Do you believe she is intellectually limited genetically? Does his racial background limit his intellectual capacity? How does his dyslexia affect his learning? Can children of blue-collar Dominican-born citizens be as smart as the upper-class Irish American kids from the suburbs? Can Black boys from poor urban families compete academically with the Jewish middle-class urban boys? Is it possible for those immigrant girls from Somalia, now in a bilingual education program, to be as smart as those Asian girls from Chinatown? Can this child with Attention Deficit Disorder (ADD) catch up with his classmates and graduate to middle school?

These are tough questions to answer. I will use the framework for attaining cultural competence, described in Chapter 3, to help you begin a dialogue with yourself about this topic. Keep in mind that *what you believe* about intelligence and achievement heavily influences your thinking, expectations, and interactions with each child.

FIRST: *Reflections.* Think about your definition of intelligence. Now, based on your definition, recall how you organize your class for learning.

1. Do you separate students by "ability"—permanently, or temporarily—until they advance to the next academic level?
2. Does the separation differentiate children by gender, race, ethnicity, physical or mental capacity, or some other category?
3. Do you separate students by "ability" based on *your* beliefs about intelligence, or because you were asked to do so by someone else? Or are you operating on automatic pilot with this decision because this is what you have always done?
4. Are your lesson plans developed on the basis of your perceptions of the intellectual development or "abilities" of your children?

SECOND: *Knowledge and Beliefs.* Think about the basic knowledge you have about intellectual development. Now, think of what *you* actually *believe* about it.

1. On what basis did you separate the children?
2. What are your beliefs about children who are performing at different levels?
3. Did you really have enough data about the childrens' study habits, skill development, test scores, strengths and weaknesses, etc., to separate them by "abilities" or any other category?
4. Can you explain to parents your rationale for their children's academic grouping?

THIRD: *Network and Resources.* Suppose several parents challenge your placement of their children.

1. What resources do you draw from to support your decision or assist you in exploring new strategies to assess how children are learning?
2. Is it appropriate to ask the principal or team leader to support your decisions, or just ask them for advice?

3. What is the district's policy on achievement testing and placement by "ability"?

FOURTH: *Change Process.* Questions about your practices or policies usually trigger questions about changing—involuntarily in this situation, since it was raised by parents. And there is always the potential for conflict.

1. Are you comfortable enough with your ideas or beliefs about intelligence, assessment, and achievement to manage these questions without undue conflict or contemplating big changes in the way you work?
2. What other types of evaluations can you use to assess what the children know?

Grappling with the topic of intelligence, and the questions posed through using the framework, will help you become more conscious of your beliefs about the intelligence of children in general, and about dominated and oppressed groups in particular. Remember that our goal is achievement for all; therefore, to determine whether you believe all children can achieve, I think it is important to examine your ideas about intelligence, because they influence your expectations of how children learn. Expectations communicated to students can determine how hard they will work to achieve. The teacher's beliefs about children's intelligence influence the type of expectations communicated (high or low) and these expectations heavily influence children's belief and behavior concerning what they can achieve. I believe this pattern exists in many school settings, and warrants further examination.

Too often reliance solely on data from standardized tests and the American belief in fixed intelligence relegates generation after generation of children in at-risk situations to years of low expectations, uninspired teaching, and disillusionment with schools. In this chapter, I will review how schools traditionally evaluate children's intelligence, explore the definition of intelligence and how it is represented in the teaching and evaluation of children, especially those in at-risk situations, and discuss how expectations of children are influenced by beliefs about their intelligence. I believe that exploring these three areas will provide more insights into working more effectively with children in culturally diverse classrooms. Let's first examine how standardized tests are used in assessing intelligence.

Standardized Testing

How do schools determine children's intellectual capabilities? Usually through some form of assessment, often national standardized tests, such as the Stanford Binet or Wechsler Intelligence Scale for Children (WISC), which are used to determine development in intelligence and are ultimately used for placement of a child within a class or by grade. History tells us that although school systems typically use these tests in this way, *they were designed as diagnostic measures* to assist in a child's development—*not to place a child in a permanent ability category.* Actually, intelligence tests such as the Binet or WISC are not usually administered to children unless they are referred for testing because a learning problem has been observed. Individual intelligence tests such as these are rather expensive to administer, and so most schools rely on achievement tests, which generate group results that can help a school determine its level of improvement or which serve as a means of self-evaluation for the school. Achievement tests, such as the California Achievement Test and Iowa Test of Basic Skills, for example, test children's knowledge in subject areas that help educators determine grade levels and growth as they relate to national norms. Achievement test results are of great interest to the general public and are thought to reflect how well a school is educating its children. Test results have particular implications in terms of the school's curriculum, teaching practices, academic standards, and per pupil expenditure.

State and district assessments are designed by local educators, often with help from national experts or local professionals deemed competent to determine how much children are learning and whether they are performing at grade level based on state norms. Superintendents are under unusual pressure to produce high scores on achievement tests to indicate that the academic program of the school system is faring well. Poor or mediocre results on achievement tests can lead to district policies and practices that influence teaching to the tests, not to the regular curriculum, and not based on the needs of the children.

Critics of achievement tests, such as early childhood expert Constance Kamii, decry use of these tests at early ages because children's development is so uneven in the first few years of life— they learn to walk, talk, write and read at different rates. Kamii highly recommends no achievement testing before third grade, and like an increasing number of educators believes that giving achievement tests just once to determine a child's progress is problematic:

> To evaluate a child's intellectual progress we should compare his or her knowledge at one point in time with the knowledge at another point in time. The interval between the two points may be one year, six months or six weeks. However, the use of achievement tests involves the comparison of children at only one point in time. Whether scores are reported in stanines, percentiles, or grade levels, these numbers are derived from comparisons of numbers of correct answers given by children of the same grade level at one point in time. (1990, p. 34)

The stigma for those who do not perform well, and the pressure for teachers to teach to the test to attain higher scores, hurts children and tends to compromise the best instructional practices. "Achievement tests are made so that half of the children at any grade level will, by definition, come out below the average. The children who come out below the average are those who are developing more slowly than the others for a variety of reasons. . . . Because achievement tests are designed to make half of the children come out below the average, they include many questions that only small percentages of children answer correctly" (Kamii, 1990, p. 34). Such testing is complicated in many districts because the texts from which the questions were derived are not the texts that are used in every district, but usually the largest ones. Therefore, with different curricula at the national and local level, it is not easy to judge how well children are learning.

Raising these few questions about achievement tests should give you pause when determining how to evaluate children in general, but particularly children in at-risk situations. For example, many children from poor homes have limited exposure to books, so their general knowledge of common words and experiences can be far different from those children who have had regular exposure to books that enrich their vocabulary and knowledge of concepts and places. Yet all too often, low performance on achievement tests gets translated as having low ability. One of my students, a reading specialist, told our class of her work five years ago as coordinator of a reading program in a rural Northeastern school district so poor that at least half the kindergartners had never seen a book or a pencil. How would these children perform on a standardized test even six months into the school year? Or how do you measure the growth of a child with Attention Deficit Disorder on an achievement test? These questions help us think about alternative measures of achievement, force us to think creatively about how to help children learn, which will result in their attaining higher scores— as opposed to teaching to the test.

And then there are those unscientific assessments that educators make based on their "beliefs" about a child's socio-economic status, parents' employment, siblings' reputation—all of which influence the teacher's expectations about the child's performance. Though these assessments are difficult to admit to ourselves at times, it is widely known that these types of assessments go on continuously in schools, fair or not. These practices raise the question of how teachers' beliefs about intelligence are formed, and how teachers come to believe in a particular theory.

Defining Intelligence

Intelligence Quotient (IQ) tests evolved in the United States and became associated with schools because the French psychologist Alfred Binet designed a test in 1905 to help teachers determine appropriate levels of instruction for children. These tests were diagnostic in nature and were designed to measure linguistic ability, logical-mathematical ability, and spacial ability and, as stated earlier, were used to assess a child's intellectual competence for appropriate instruction—not for permanent placement or rating of intellectual capacity for life. Later, the major debate among psychologists centered on whether general intelligence occupied a major region of the mind (Spearman, 1927) or several primary mental abilities were located in different regions of the mind (Thurstone, 1938). There has been disagreement on how to define intelligence among psychologists and other professionals for decades, and the debate continues. For example, the arguments some of us are familiar with include where the locus of intelligence lies. Is it within the individual, is it within the environment, or is intelligence within the interaction between the individual and the environment? (Sternberg & Detterman, 1986). There are biological approaches that tell us that intelligence is in the brain and that brain activity related to the nervous system, brain size, and hemispheric specialization influences intelligence; the cognitive approach tells us that there are mental representations that define intelligence, and that perhaps verbal and mathematical abilities are the major indicator of intelligence; the contextual approach describes how intelligence cannot be defined outside a particular environmental and cultural context; and the systems approach offers an integration of the context and the cognitive (Sternberg, 1988). *There is much more to understanding the different approaches, but my point is that most of us have adopted a view put forth by someone else or the one espoused by the system, without serious consideration of whether it is what* **we** *believe, based on careful analysis. So why are we so resistant to even considering changing our perspective if doing so can help our children?*

As teachers we must be accountable to ourselves first, and stay attuned to the principles and values of importance to us. We may have to learn how to work within a system that might operate with a different set of principles, but we must be conscious of both our own principles and those of the system in order to justify what we do in class for ourselves and for our students. In a less complex world, school administrators would not knowingly ask educators to participate in untoward practices that might violate their principles; however, only individually can we determine if this actually happens.

Careful examination of our own beliefs and principles is necessary before we can make such comparisons. This level of consciousness about what you believe and how you behave simply cannot be avoided if you are serious about moving toward cultural competence to help all children achieve at high levels.

According to Ducette, Sewell, and Shapiro (1996), there had been no real challenge in the fields of psychology and education to the IQ and other standardized tests of cognitive development until 1983, when Howard Gardner and his colleagues introduced MI— Multiple Intelligences Theory. Gardner reviewed his theory in a recent issue of *Educational Leadership*:

> The standard view of intelligence is that intelligence is something you are born with; you have only a certain amount of it; you cannot do much about how much of that intelligence you have; and tests exist that can tell you how smart you are. The theory of multiple intelligences challenges that view. It asks instead, "Given what we know about the brain, evolution, and the differences in cultures, what are the sets of human abilities we all share?" My analysis suggested that rather than one or two intelligences, all human beings have several (eight) intelligences. What makes life interesting, however, is that we don't have the same strength in each intelligence area, and we don't have the same amalgam of intelligences. Just as we look different from one another and have different personalities, we also have different kinds of minds. (Checkley, 1997, p. 9)

Gardner further reveals that the implications for teaching are enormous, because using his theory means that practitioners need no longer to cater *solely* to the language-logic profile of intelligence that the IQ tests and other ability tests are based on. It means that teachers can create other instructional options to engage students in learning, and can assist students in using their combination of intelligences. The eight intelligences defined by Gardner and his colleagues include: linguistic, logical-mathematical, spatial, bodily kinesthetic, musical, interpersonal, intrapersonal, and naturalistic, each having unique and discernible characteristics that distinguish it from the others.

This type of theory also addresses what some critics believe are culturally biased standardized tests—tests that are based on one set of standards, ways of living, and norms based on a middle-class, European lifestyle. This type of test would place at a disadvantage students with different cultural backgrounds, socio-economic status, a different learning style, or different values. The popularity and wide use of Gardner's theory of intelligence is a testament to educators' interest in finding ways for more children to succeed. Perhaps it is also an acknowledgment of the limits of standardized tests and their use, and an incentive to move beyond teaching to the tests as a means of helping children improve academically. Multiple Intelligences Theory (MI Theory) is radically different from IQ tests because Gardner and his colleagues argue that not only are the current eight intelligences independent of each other, but many of them cannot be measured by traditional standardized tests.

More important to our conversation is the fact that the measurement of intelligence according to MI Theory is more dependent on authentic assessments, such as portfolios and curricula activities as a base for determining problem-solving skills, as opposed to standardized tests. Another advantage for children with diverse backgrounds is the variety of intelligences that offer new ways for educators to view a child's success. For example, there is musical intelligence and linguistic intelligence as well as the traditional spatial intelligence and logical-mathematical intelligence. *The point in sharing the difference in traditional measures of intelligence and a new one is to demonstrate that there is more than one type of measure available, and to trigger your thinking about what measures you believe inform your understanding of a child's achievement.*

A Recommendation

Allow me to first introduce a concept about intelligence that makes sense to me because I can identify with the reasoning—I believe it will make sense to you; and, second, let me share a definition of intelligence that can encompass use of standardized tests and other measures of cognitive functioning. First, the concept: *It is the idea that intelligence tests do not measure the full range of intellectual functioning, such as insight or practical abilities.* Sternberg (1988) also demonstrates with this example that behaviors considered "smart" in testing situations, are in fact "not so smart" in real life.

> Psychologists have found that a *reflective* cognitive
> style is generally associated with greater intelligence
> than is a *compulsive* style. Jumping to conclusions
> without adequate reflection can often lead to false
> starts and erroneous conclusions. In making pur-
> chases we can often save a tidy sum by shopping
> around first. Of course there are some people, such
> as air traffic controllers, who must make important
> split-second decisions as part of their jobs. But most
> of us encounter few significant problems in our work
> or personal lives that do not warrant some time for
> reflection. (p. 23)

*But it is a common belief that quickness is an attribute of intel-
ligence.* Wait time is something that few teachers use as a teaching
or learning tool, so they quickly assume that a child does not know
an answer if she or he does not respond fast enough. What many
psychologists have found is that "What is critical is not speed per
se but, speed selection—knowing when and when not to perform
tasks rapidly" (p. 23). It is very important that you not make assumptions about intelligence, or assume that others know what a
child can or cannot do, *without some investigation of your own.* Think
about it: you and the child will have a new, different relationship in
a new environment, and you may be able to make even greater
progress than the teacher before you. It is imperative that you re-
frain from beginning your relationship with a child highlighting
intellectual or other deficits, based *solely* on past test performance.

Second, I would commend to you Robert Sternberg's triarchic
theory of intelligence because it makes sense and recognizes intelligence in more than one way. Sternberg (1988), a renowned Yale
University psychologist, has studied and written about intelligence,
thinking, and problem solving for over two decades. He believes
that most standardized tests measure a very limited set of abilities and that intelligence is more than a narrow set of abilities.
"Mental self-management of one's life in a constructive, purposeful
way" (p. 11) is how he defines intelligence. He goes on to define his
triarchic (three-part) theory.

> First, according to this theory, intelligence serves
> three functions in real-world contexts. The first, ad-

aptation to the environment, refers to people's changing of themselves in order to suit the environments
in which they live. The second, shaping of environment, refers to people's changing of their environments to suit themselves. And the third, selection of
environments, refers to people's choosing new environments when they are unable to make their environments work for them either through adaptation
or shaping . . . according to the triarchic theory. Environments and the tasks we confront within them vary
in terms of their familiarity. At one extreme, we have
tasks within environments that are extremely novel
and that we have never before encountered. At the
other extreme we have tasks that are so familiar that
we accomplish them almost without thinking. (p. 282)

Though this theory is different from Gardner's, there is simi-
larity between Gardner's idea that each person is not equally strong
in each intelligence and Sternberg's idea that some things one can
do automatically without thinking—a strength, while others are
novel and seldom encountered—a challenge, or an area of less
strength initially.

Each of the elements Sternberg proposes raise important questions about how we function in everyday life, but not all are found
on achievement tests. We have to use intelligence in functioning in
many settings; learning where our strengths and weaknesses are
can help us understand ourselves and where we need to improve.
Teachers can do the same with students, learning their strengths
and weaknesses through a variety of measures (including standardized tests), and by defining intelligence in more broad terms.
What really matters in our efforts to help students achieve is what
we believe and how we interpret, communicate, and use the results
from any measures designed to determine how well students are
learning. Therefore, being conscious and clear about what you believe is a critically important matter for you and your students.

Intelligence, Feedback, and Teacher Efficacy

The reality of school life is that some form of standardized testing
will be used to assess children's achievement, and teachers must

learn how to use them to a student's advantage. The issue is not avoiding standardized tests, but how you use them with other measures, such as teacher-designed tests, portfolios, and the like to assess a child's academic growth. Another word that describes the data from the tests is feedback. Feedback is information that reveals enough about a situation to assist one in redesigning a strategy for improvement, or to reinforce a strategy that is working. The Iowa Test of Basic Skills, the Stanford 9, and other achievement tests are divided into categories of skills and grade levels to assist in interpreting a child's strengths and weaknesses. The feedback can support a teacher's plan to help each child. Grade level curriculum, feedback from standardized tests, and data from the children's classwork can be useful in understanding how a child is performing and in developing a plan to move the children forward academically, not to "peg" them as having high or low ability.

You and your colleagues can devise ways of building on what children know to ultimately arrive at what they have yet to learn. Use the tests as a diagnostic tool, instead of as a definitive statement of the child's "ability." Using tests to determine "ability" becomes a self-fulfilling prophecy, because both the teacher and the student give up before they get started. Besides, there may be some insurmountable hurdles to overcome if, for example, the state curriculum is out of alignment with that on which the national test was normed; even greater problems may arise if teachers are not given the training or explanations for interpreting the tests to discern why their children did well or poorly on the tests. You must be able to explain to yourself, families, and other educators (such as next year's teacher) what you did to move the children forward academically—not why they cannot function because of their weaknesses. The following example demonstrates what a school can do to use its test scores with other measures of achievement for an urban, poor population.

In this elementary school of primarily immigrant children, 55 percent of the first and second graders, and over 60 percent of the third and fourth graders scored at Level 1 in Reading on the Stanford 9 Early School Achievement Test. Level 1 is defined as little or no mastery in Reading. This baseline data was worse than any of the educators in the system had imagined, even though they were aware that the majority of children came from poor neighborhoods where a majority of the children live in homes where a language other than English is the primary home language. The good news was that close to 15 percent in each grade scored at Level 3 in Reading, defined as solid academic performance and readiness for the next grade, with some grades having between 2 and 4 percent of students scoring at Level 4, signifying superior performance. But the great news was that 70 percent of the all-day kindergartners (from the same neighborhoods), who received close to 3 hours of language instruction daily, scored at Level 3, indicating solid performance for the next grade. After feeling distressed and a little depressed, the principal and superintendent decided to call a meeting of the teachers to explain the feedback—the meaning of the scores and their implication for their ongoing work during the school year.

After acknowledging their initial disappointment, they explained the scores, and shared the implications of the low scores and the few high ones students earned. Then they asked for reactions before launching into a brainstorming session on how they would improve the performance of the students. Here are some examples of the teachers' questions, and suggestions from their joint session:

- show us the total breakdown of scores by grade, so we can examine the greatest area of weakness and strength (vocabulary, reading comprehension, etc.),
- formalize the request to the school board for that reading specialist some of us requested last year,
- compare and examine our current teacher-based evaluations against those used on the standardized tests,
- compare our curricula against that of the standardized test,
- what is different about the instructional practices of the kindergartners?
- compare our lesson plans and find out what works best in each grade, so the best strategies can be shared and interpreted for appropriate grade levels,
- focus more on certain reading skills in all our other subject areas to give students even more time in reading,

- build more reading into the after-school program's homework clinic, and bring in volunteers to read with the classes,
- invite older students who read well to practice with younger students as a community service project on the week-ends and after school,
- find out what other schools have done in similar situations to avoid spending time reinventing successful programs that already exist, and
- discuss our own skills in reading and obtain more help through staff development training if necessary.

Some teachers were overwhelmed and worried about how the children could get to grade level by the end of the year, but the principal asked that they set challenging goals and continue to analyze students' progress through classroom observations, quizzes and class tests and their usual school measures. She would provide them with current research on academic gains in reading given certain programs and strategies, but that each teacher must strive to ensure measurable gains with each child and continue to get the children excited and motivated to read. The educators focused on what they could do first, then began moving outward to specialists, volunteers, and other school systems. Though they were worried about how to move the students faster, no one blamed the children. What could be gained from blaming the children anyway?

In my judgment, teachers have a special responsibility to discover each child's strengths. *How you interpret strengths and weaknesses makes a big difference to the child in question; if you interpret the student deficiencies or weaknesses as limitations based on intelligence, then teacher interventions to improve performance are limited because the child is viewed as not having ability.* Explaining what you did to capitalize on the child's growth is also necessary. When children enter your classroom, one of your goals is to assist the child's growth and development *while in your care.* Giving up on a child, or planning only limited activities, or assuming how much or how little the child will progress based on a test score or previous experience suggests that teachers cannot make a difference in a student's performance because of his or her innate intellectual capacity.

Children, especially children in at-risk situations, come to school to learn, to grow, and to improve themselves under your tutelage—not to have teachers or systems continuously set up roadblocks based on limited perceptions about test scores and intelligence. They come for help, support, nurturance and, yes, HOPE. Do you have the right to dash a child's enthusiasm for learning? Herbert Kohl, a celebrated teacher of over 30 years, champion of poor children, author and humanitarian, declares in his latest book, *The Discipline of Hope* (1998), "Providing hope to young people is the major challenge of teaching" (p. 9). How can teachers provide that hope? *By remembering that the child sees you first and you represent his school experience more than anyone else.* So the caring, hopeful, positive communication about learning must come from you first. Teachers who believe that what they do in class makes a difference in a child's performance are said to have a high sense of efficacy (Weber and Omotani, 1994). Teacher efficacy has been a topic of much research since the early 1980s when Ashton, Webb, and Doda (1983) and Gibson and Dembo (1984) conducted studies, after extensive literature reviews on teaching that particularly focused on how teachers believed they could influence students' learning. These researchers learned that there are several differences between high- and low-efficacy teachers, and that teacher effectiveness is directly tied to teacher efficacy.

Ashton, Webb, and Doda (1983) found that: "Teachers with high efficacy attitudes tended to maintain high academic standards, concentrate on academic instruction, monitor students' on-task behavior, and develop a warm, supportive classroom environment, and their students had higher achievement test scores than students of teachers with low-efficacy attitudes" (p. 4). Teachers with high-efficacy attitudes were even able to maintain these attitudes with low-achieving students, unlike teachers with low-efficacy attitudes. In this early exploratory study, low-efficacy teachers had different expectations of and relationships with children: "Teachers with low-efficacy attitudes tended to sort and stratify their classes according to ability and give preferential treatment (more instruction, more appropriate praise and feedback, more interaction, more assignments) to high ability students" (p. v). Low-efficacy teachers have low expectations for low-performing students, blame students, their parents, and circumstances for poor performance, tend not to build working relationships with students, and often see them as threatening, do not carefully monitor students' work, and are convinced that there is not much they can do to affect the outcome of the children's performance, implying a belief in fixed intelligence.

These low-efficacy teachers have a negative impact on a child's interest in learning, and contribute to the sense of hopelessness and failure exhibited by students in at-risk situations. Yet teacher efficacy is a variable akin to a person's confidence and can be influenced by the environment, relationships, and beliefs about student achievement (Fletcher, 1990; Tracz & Gibson, 1986). This means teacher efficacy is not necessarily a stable attribute; it can be influenced by both external variables, such as environment (climate of school, quality of relationships with supervisors, peers, and parents), and internal variables, such as beliefs (about student achievement and behavior, or personal ability to control what happens in class). I believe that controlling internal factors, that is, what you believe about yourself and what you believe about students' *capabilities* to learn, is the first step toward becoming a high-efficacy teacher.

Because they are the casualties of ineffective teaching practices, misused and misinterpreted standardized test scores, allegiance to the idea of fixed intelligence and plain old outdated, one-dimensional, teacher-centered pedagogy, millions of children are placed at-risk of failing and dropping out of school every year. Experienced and novice educators alike must understand that they cannot use the same traditional pedagogy they learned in teacher education programs that do not work for all children, and that they must become as creative as the faculty and staff of dozens of successful programs in which diverse learners are improving and in many schools are already excelling. Different students in new eras demand different approaches, practices, and educational structures to meet the demands of their times. To be more effective with all students, educators can no longer blindly accept practices and policies that work against the optimal development of some of the children. We must actively seek out solutions to challenging learning situations, assess the validity of our current practices, and begin to examine ourselves and the educational institutions we work in.

At some point in your career, you are accountable for your work with children in at-risk situations; you may not be responsible for total educational reform, but you will be accountable for making reasonable attempts to improve the academic life of children. Working with other educators who believe that each child has the capacity to learn, and with families and community members, is critical to ensuring a sound education for children in the best of circumstances, and is imperative for children in at-risk situations. Let us continue to explore another concern related to intelligence—teacher expectations.

Expectations

How you define and measure your students' intelligence and what you believe about their current level of functioning—fixed or not—will impact their achievement in school. Tied very closely to a teacher's belief about a child's intelligence is whether there is a communication of high or low expectations of a child's performance in school. How and what teachers communicate about expectations have a great impact on whether a student is engaged in learning at all. Study after study has confirmed that students will live up to the expectations set for them (Rist, 1970; Rosenthal, 1974), and that students at risk are often victims of low expectations from their teachers and other adults in their lives.

Jeff Howard, a social psychologist, has created a training model for educators at his Efficacy Institute, an educational consulting organization known for working with urban schools. His work is built on the thesis that by communicating low expectations and implying that certain children are not smart, we undermine their confidence, which he believes is their energy for working hard. His model for understanding this is as follows:

Confidence → Effective Effort → Development

Building confidence is the key not only to assure greater development in children, but it is also the fuel for teacher efficacy—believing in their capacity to teach all children. Like more and more of his contemporaries, Howard has believed for many years that the innate ability theory of intelligence is inappropriate for explaining the lack of performance and achievement of so many of America's children. He explains his position:

> People are obviously not born with the same talents, in the same measure, but it is reasonable and prudent for us to assume that the great majority of our children, too, are endowed enough to achieve verbal and mathematical competence . . . We need a new approach to education . . . a new framework with an empowering idea of what development is . . . *It is a process of building capacity.* In a new educational paradigm, the most important single factor controlling the learning capacity of children is a characteristic of adults: the ability to view development as a process that we have the power to manage. Taking responsibility for the development of children depends on willfully breaking the line, in our own minds, between a child's learning capacity and crude measures of intelligence. *All children can learn if the process of learning is effectively organized and managed by adults.* (1990, p. 11)

If Howard's premise is accurate, it will be difficult to blame the children for not achieving well in schools. At the very least, educators can test the programs described by Howard and others to support their efforts with children in at-risk situations. Communicating positive expectations is one way to influence students to work hard, believe in themselves, and to perform at a high level.

Are you brave enough to take on the challenge of suspending disbelief about a student's intelligence as the problem, and place on hold the innate ability model, while you experiment with another approach to reach children at risk of failing in your schools? Don't you owe it to the children and parents for whom you work to use all your resources to help the children achieve? Are you only a teacher for those children who came to you already demonstrating high capabilities? Do you have any special responsibility to help children who are not performing at grade level, to close the gap between their current performance level and grade level performance? Here is a personal story about my training at Efficacy that might influence how you answer these questions.

During my second year as a trainer with the Efficacy Institute, I was scheduled for a five-day training with 25 teachers from five elementary schools in a large, mid-western inner-city system. During the second day, two very dedicated third grade teachers had described their frustration at inheriting a small number of third graders who could barely read at the first grade level. With over 25 students in each class, they had difficulty providing enough individual attention to help these students improve to the point where they would have a fighting chance to keep up with the class. They were impressed with the Efficacy Model of Development, and decided to work together on increasing the reading level of three students in each of their classes during the month before the next training session. Participants were asked to think of a nagging problem to solve using the information they had learned so far, and to set challenging but realistic goals to work on during the month we were apart. Each person was assigned a partner for support and encouragement to reinforce her new knowledge. The third grade teachers decided that they would attempt to get three of their students who read at the first grade level to complete a familiar second grade book that complemented the formal second grade textbook. It was described as a colorful, fun book to read and one that most second graders enjoyed very much. After the training resumed a month later, the two teachers could hardly contain themselves as the report about the results of the goal setting were revealed. They had to report first!

The teachers described how they enlisted the help of the parents, described the challenge to the students, explaining that the work would be fun, but that they had to work especially hard and would be given extra assistance in class during the time the other students were doing independent reading. What the teachers were most thrilled about was how excited, involved, and focused the children were, particularly after communicating their belief that the children could meet the challenge. They reported that the children exhibited a more positive attitude in all their work, but especially toward reading. The children seemed like different people and seemed to thrive on the attention they received, even though the work was remedial. One teacher was able to get all three of her students to complete the book; the other teacher was able to get two of her three students to finish the book during the same amount of time. The third child took only one more week to complete the book.

The reported bonus for these teachers was how invigorated and empowered *they* felt after having orchestrated the children's meeting the goals. Their sense of efficacy about teaching children below grade level in reading had given them such a boost that they were sure they could do the same for others in their classes. They left the seminar determined to get those three children up to reading at grade level by the end of the school year.

What happened in this example demonstrates the energy and confidence that can be communicated when teachers believe in students and use appropriate strategies and tools to meet their goals. Notice that the teachers engaged the students in the process, communicated belief and confidence in them, and provided support at school and at home. A win-win situation results because when the teaching-learning process is orchestrated well, it is mutually beneficial for teachers and children.

Ask yourself the questions in the Diversity Notebook, then work on the attitudes, beliefs, and knowledge of your trusted colleagues. Together you can design a way to begin communicating more effectively with the children and ultimately initiate communication with the administrators responsible for assisting in these endeavors.

Summary Questions **Diversity and Achievement**
A.   Am I able to explain my beliefs about the intelligence of children who are not making satisfactory progress in my class?
B.   What activities can I engage in with my colleagues to keep me open to reading feedback without trying to fit new information into concepts I already know?
C.   What questions do I need to ask myself to stay conscious about the level of expectations I hold for my students?
D.   What obstacles exist in the school structure or policies that might impede the progress of children at risk of failing?

Diversity Notebook

A.   Review Scenario A below. You have been selected by your peers to organize a committee to address the concerns raised by the increasingly diverse student population. Outline your plans to address the concerns cited, using some of the ideas described thus far.

Scenario A. In a suburban town an hour's drive from a major inner city, the school population is no longer predominately white; close to 55 percent are a mix of African American, Cambodian, Chinese, Portuguese, and Hispanic, primarily Dominican. The teachers are predominately white in all the schools (elementary, middle and secondary), and there has been a growing division among them about how to address their concerns about the different behaviors of the students, in class and out. None of the new diverse groups are enrolled in college-bound programs, except the Chinese, and the racial incidents and misunderstandings among students and staff seem to increase each year. Parents of the new students have complained of the unfair treatment their children have received in class and during extra-curricular activities. Tension is high among staff, and there seems to be little leadership from principals or the school committee to address their concerns.

B.   Review Scenario B below. Imagine yourself as the teacher of the class who has to meet with the parents inquiring about programs for the gifted and talented. Develop a strategy for addressing their concerns, and set the agenda for the meeting.

Scenario B. A Black elementary school teacher in an inner-city school is distressed to learn that the parents of the two white children and the three Arab American children have asked for a meeting to discuss concerns about the progress of their children in her class. The other 20 children in her class are Black. She wonders how these families came together and what these "concerns" are. Later she learns from the principal that one of the concerns of the families is about accelerated, or gifted, programs for their children; at least one family has discussed transferring out of the school if these programs cannot be provided.

References

Ashton, P., Webb, R. B., & Doda, N. A. (1983). *A study of teachers' sense of efficacy: Final report.* Washington, DC: National Institute of Education, U.S. Department of Education.

Checkley, K. (1997). The first seven . . . and the eighth: A conversation with Howard Gardner. *Educational Leadership* 55(1), 8–13.

Ducette, J. P., Sewell, T. E., & Shapiro, J. P. (1996). *Diversity in education: Problems and possibilities.* In Frank B. Murray (Ed.), *The teacher educator's handbook* (pp. 323–380). San Francisco: Jossey-Bass.

Fletcher, S. (1990). *The relation of school environment to teacher efficacy.* Paper presented at the annual meeting of the American Psychological Association Meeting, Boston, MA. (ERIC Document Reproductive Service No. ED 329 551).

Gibson, S., & Dembo, M. (1984). Teacher efficacy: A construct validation. *Journal of Educational Psychology,* 76(4), 569–582.

Howard, J. (1990). *Getting smart: The social construction of intelligence.* Lexington, MA: The Efficacy Institute.

Kamii, C. (Ed.) (1990). *Achievement testing in the early grades.* Washington, DC: National Association of Young Children.

Kohl, H. (1998). *The discipline of hope.* New York: Simon & Schuster.

Rist, R. C. (1970). Student social class and teacher expectation. *Harvard Educational Review* 40(3), 411–451.

Rosenthal, R. (1974). Pygmalion effects: What you expect is what you get. *Psychology Today Cassette, 12.* New York: Ziff-Davis.

Spearman, C. (1927). *The abilities of man.* New York: Macmillan.

Sternberg, R. J. (Ed.) (1988). *Handbook of human intelligence.* Cambridge: Cambridge University Press.

Sternberg, R. J., & Detterman, D. K. (Eds.) (1986). *What is intelligence?* Norwood, NJ: Ablex.

Thurstone, L. L. (1938). Primary mental abilities. *Psychometic Monographs,* I (a).

Tracz, S. M., & Gibson, S. (1986). *Effects of efficacy on academic achievement.* (Reports-Research/Technical [143], 8p; Paper presented at the annual meeting of the California Educational Research Association, Marina del Ray, CA, November 13–14, 1986). (ERIC Document Reproductive Service No. ED 281 853).

Weber, B. J., & Omotani, L. M. (1994). The power of believing. *Executive Educator,* 16(9), 35–38.

CHAPTER 5

Moving Toward Cultural Competence

It is time to begin using the concepts and framework presented in the first four chapters. I believe the most important concepts to understand, as you move toward enhancing your work with diverse populations, are those that influence children's confidence and their capacity to learn. Children's characteristics or human differences, such as race, gender or exceptionality, are often seen as the major problem, but you must learn to analyze a problem by looking beyond the obvious in order to determine the true challenge. To demonstrate *educational care for each child*, as Dr. Levine described it in Chapter 2, we must seek the source of the circumstances that prevent the child from functioning optimally. And we do this in part by building on the child's strengths, advocating for her or him, and working out a plan to manage difficulties that arise. This means planning, and not jumping to conclusions that are based on simple observations.

For example, one of the more common occurrences in culturally and racially diverse settings is the response to witnessing a fight between two children of obviously different races. Many children and adults would automatically assume that the fight happened because of some conflict about their racial differences. Not necessarily. That is certainly one possibility, but we cannot make such assumptions without an investigation of what really happened and hearing from the children and persons who witnessed the event.

Respecting each child's rights, and analyzing each encounter with as much objectivity as possible, is expected of someone who reflects regularly on what is happening in school. Children are very observant little people, and our behavior is always up for scrutiny regarding fairness in our encounters with them. How you handle a social conflict in the hallways will forecast for a child how you might handle an academic concern. A quick review of the framework is in order before we work through a couple of scenarios. This means starting with reflections on your professional behavior.

Personal Reflections

Reflections about your vision for teaching, expectations of yourself and of each child will guide your behavior in your interactions with children from diverse backgrounds, too. Staying connected to your role as a teacher and the vision and goals you have set for yourself is what will help you stay balanced. Keeping a sense of balance will help you maintain your perspective in difficult circumstances, and will help you become strong enough to be open to considering new or different alternatives to solving problems, especially with children in at-risk situations.

If you cannot engage in honest self-reflection, and cannot be part of a team to develop reflective practices to improve your teaching, then your success with diverse populations—who often require innovation and experimentation with non-traditional strategies—will be limited. Practice in self-reflection may be your first step in managing the diversity in your classroom.

Thinking more about the instructional decisions you make and the basis on which you make them can become a regular habit that can spawn new ideas and strategies that you might not think of otherwise. Regular means daily, weekly or monthly. Too many of us claim to be too busy to do this. Some decisions may seem to be made automatically because of what you might routinely do for a more homogenous group of children—who share many micro-cultures. But will this routine work if there is greater heterogeneity of micro-cultures, which brings new and different perspectives to the classroom? For example, should you have a child in class who uses a wheelchair, you are forced to think about your seating pattern, his comfort in the chair, his mobility in class; what happens in case of a fire drill; creating a climate of acceptance for him in the class; and a host of other socio-cultural issues that affect how he learns and how you teach. What adjustments can you make on your own, and which ones will you need help with? Being conscious and aware of how you make decisions for any child will guide you in this new situation, as well. Staying connected to who you are and why teaching is important to you has great benefits and can be quite satisfying. Symbols of who you are and what you believe should be noticeable in your classroom, in the relationships you have with your children, and, for example, in the comfort and progress of that child in the wheelchair who is so well-adjusted in your classroom now.

Dr. Pamela Gerloff (1997), an educator and author, wrote an article called the "Power of Self-Connections," in which she refers to this connection that educators need with themselves to work more effectively with children in at-risk situations: "In each of us there is a space or state of awareness where we feel completely safe, completely powerful, completely protected, and completely content. It is from this space of awareness that our unique life purpose, our destiny, our deepest longing and our greatest joy arise" (p. 122). In other words, this means connecting to who you really are—not a role you play for others. There should be congruence between who you say you are and what you do that is recognizable by all who know you. In his book, *The Courage to Teach* (1998), Parker Palmer describes this role we sometimes play as a type of dividedness. "Pretending is another name for dividedness, a state that keeps us from cultivating the capacity for connectedness on which good teaching depends. When we pretend, we fall out of community with ourselves, our students, and the world around us, out of communion with the common center that is both the root and the fruit of teaching at its best" (p. 86). Sometimes we pretend things are fine when we know they are not, yet we refuse to take the time to sort them out. If we put off addressing the pretense often enough and long enough, pretty soon we have convinced ourselves that the pretense is how we really feel about a topic, and thus begins the path to dividedness of which Palmer speaks.

Connecting to ourselves about some of the tough issues, such as the (1) disproportionate numbers of boys assigned to special education, the alarmingly high percentage of African-American boys who are disciplined more than any other child in schools across the nation (Banks & Banks, 1997), (2) disproportionate numbers of second language learners in the bottom ranks of academic classes across the nation, and (3) neglected special education of gifted or accelerated children that is all but ignored in most states, means we must make time to think about these issues, and give them enough attention so we do not continue to perpetrate these disastrous conditions on our children! The irony is that pretending also takes energy and time. Though working through these issues may slow down your pace for awhile, your overall goals for all the children will be more fully met. When learning about a new challenge for one different child, it is rare that you do not learn something for the benefit of the whole group. For example, the teacher who searched for interactive computer games for his third graders who were shy and embarrassed about speaking the little English they knew in class, found interactive games in other subject areas that would augment his lesson plans for all his children. What a coincidence! **When you stay connected to yourself and your vision, you are always better prepared for whatever challenges arise at school and in other parts of your life**.

When you are disconnected, you will be caught off guard much more easily, and even the routine pressures of school life will tend to overwhelm you. It is easier to lose perspective on a multitude of issues, and it is real easy to become frustrated, set in your ways, and less open to new thinking. Disconnected teachers are those who tend to say when new issues arise, "Oh, we discussed that issue five years ago, and did not get anywhere with it!" or "I know all I need to know about that!"

If you are already staying in tune with yourself, adding reflective time that is focused on your belief and your pedagogy will not be a great challenge. However, if you are among the many who have not taken much time to reconnect in months or years, it is well past time to do so—give it a try. But start small. Take a few minutes before class, during your preparation time at school, or during lunch. Some people have affirmations they read, others just review the day and remind themselves of their goals and why they are taking a certain approach to a particular problem. I have one colleague (an elementary team leader) who is so disciplined that she tapes her reflections about the day on a daily basis, in her car, in traffic, on the way from school. By doing this she can release the pent-up energy, frustration, or exhilaration of the day by herself first. Then she chooses more carefully what she shares with her partner and children when she arrives home. And since she always has homework to do, she has a second chance to think about those concerns she must address the next day. By the way, this teacher learned to do this after being offered the team leader position at her school—now she recommends it to her friends and colleagues.

Reflections with Peers

Others may develop habits of reflection with colleagues, especially when there is a problem you want help in solving. Working with someone else can be easier when you work out ways to be account-able to each other, for maintaining your reflection time, or for work-ing on a challenge in your classroom. One of my close colleagues is also my mentor, and we check in with each other every two weeks on how we are doing with our professional lives.

Another group I belong to is a mix of educators—principals, teachers, and college faculty, six of us altogether. We are all female and we meet monthly to work on a project, but inevitably the first order of business is sharing how we are doing in our positions and discussing "the issue" that challenged us since we last met. These discussions are mutually beneficial because of the diversity of our positions, knowledge, and opinions. I listen to the variety of opin-ions expressed and the challenges faced by this group, and I am awed and thankful to be a part of it. We make it fun, too, by meet-ing for dinner first.

Using part of a weekly or even monthly staff meeting to check in with your colleagues is another way to begin reflections with your peers. No matter which way you choose to stay in tune, it is important that you do it—it will serve you well as you continue to grow in the profession, and it will help you keep your sanity in such a pressured, fast-paced field. And I believe you will be at a distinct advantage when a parent, a professional colleague, or a community member interacts with you about a child in an at-risk situation; you are less likely to view the students as just another burden for you and will be more open to learning what to do to help the child succeed.

Reflecting about Pedagogy

To foster this type of a collaboration among more teachers, formal staff development programs can be designed with a similar goal in mind—to support teachers' connecting to themselves and re-aligning their thinking and behavior to make their classrooms places of achievement for all children. Proposing a staff development program may take time, especially if no process for regular staff development is in place. To keep moving, you and your colleagues can consider presenting a brief workshop on what you have learned and on how you have benefited from building the habit of reflection. Or you may choose to ask colleagues from other schools or a professional organization to introduce the subject. Small successes can be quite satisfying and can be reinforcing until more educators are involved.

Discussions about pedagogy and the curriculum are likely to be central or recurring topics of teacher reflections. Ongoing dialogue about which practices are working and which are not can naturally create a forum once the discussions have begun. The isolation that teachers are used to might make the early conversation sessions difficult to convene, but they catch fire easily when a climate of support to facilitate learning is understood, instead of one of criticism and scrutiny for selfish gains.

Sharing new practices and ideas for children performing at different levels and for culturally relevant curricula are two other related topics ripe for a teacher's agenda, especially through staff development. Acknowledgment and recognition of pedagogy that works is as important as keeping up to date on the research and theory in areas of difficulty. In this way a school faculty can retain instructional practices that work to build and integrate them with the new ones that fit with the mission and goals set by the district. Planning for the demands of teaching and the children of the future is critical now—not when you are face to face with the demands of the new century. Developing the habit of reflecting on your professional behavior can be practiced while initiating one or two of the other steps in the framework.

Examining Beliefs and Knowledge of Diverse Groups

This is the second step in the framework. This section is important because it helps us uncover some of the teaching we received from our family and communities, and can explain some of our behavior toward particular groups. According to recent studies, multiple opportunities for understanding, interacting with and learning about different groups is recommended as a means of making better decisions and developing more appropriate strategies to help children in at-risk situations (McDiarmid & Price, 1993). These can include (1) recalling how you came to your own beliefs about a particular group, and checking them against facts and current norms in society; (2) building relationships with children's families, which can teach you about their cultures, expectations for their children, or what education means to them; and (3) taking a course, conducting a little research, or doing some reading on your own to increase your knowledge about the different groups represented in your class.

Deliberately cultivating friendships with people from different cultures than your own, studying the effects of poverty on families, learning all you can about a child's mental or physical impairments or talents can add insights about how to develop appropriate programs and resources for them. Observing families as they interact and noting how they teach their children at home can lead to greater understanding of how the children adjust to learning in school. Ignoring the effects of violence, racism, sexism and discrimination on some children is to be truly ignorant of what is happening in the world in general, and their worlds in particular. In other words, knowing the environment your children live in outside of school can assist you in making a connection with them. Having better connections with them in authentic ways helps you teach in more relevant ways and promotes greater achievement from them. This is just what the teachers did in the Powell articles in Chapter 2.

Understanding the Change Process

Using this third lens forces us to address how personal our response to change is. Self-knowledge helps you separate a bonafide academic concern from your response to *just another change the system is requiring* in your school life. The C-BAM model, with its six stages of concern about change and its impact on your work just reminds you that you are human; most of us get comfortable with things as they are and find change threatening. However, given some notice, and a realistic goal, most of us can make an adjustment as long as we can make some decisions about balancing something new with all the other responsibilities, and as long as we can have some input and feel the change will truly benefit students.

Building Resources for Networking

This is the last lens that is used for analyzing the scenarios. This is probably one of the more obvious aspects of the framework, but sometimes educators do not know where to go to find relevant resources to assist them or they are reluctant to ask for help. First, find someone who is doing well with students who represent the differences you need to accommodate. Pick their brains about their resources—most folks are more than happy to help. Call professional educational associations for materials on their diversity networks, or just get the word out on the grapevine that you are interested in certain kinds of material that will provide support for your work. Ask your school specialist to recommend consultants and resources in the district who have experience with the students you are trying to serve, including families of children with similar difficulties. If you have access to the Internet, there are literally thousands of contacts you can make about supporting diverse learners.

Corporate and foundation support can be sought if funding is needed for special programs, and community institutions and organizations such as the Rotary, Boys and Girls Clubs, and other nonprofits that believe in what you are doing can often provide help. Use your imagination, and don't be afraid to ask questions—of anyone you think can help you—even the students themselves.

Scenarios

I will now work through the first scenario with you, using the relevant concepts in the book and the guidelines from the framework to begin developing strategies to solve some of the academic and social difficulties in this scenario. I will lead you into the second scenario, but leave space for you to add your own questions and recommended strategies. On the third one, I expect you to work it through to completion.

In this first scenario, a second-year teacher describes her dilemma with her fourth grade class. To facilitate processing the information in the scenario, you can use this outline as a guide:

- list the facts about the environment, the teacher, and the students
- identify the major problems
- summarize the scenario in your own words
- ask yourself questions to generate thinking about the problems
- think about how the scenario problems are similar and/or different from other school problems you have experienced
- brainstorm strategies to work through to resolve the problem

1. Rassany

It is the third week of classes, and I am finally settling into some routines with my twenty-two fourth graders. I am a little worried about some of them, especially Rassany, a Laotian American girl, who has been in America for only five years. She is an animated speaker when she is with some of the other Laotian girls, and though her English is quite limited, she can hold conversations with the other English speaking children, who seem to understand her. Her reading is on the second grade level, and her writing in English is poor. Her family refuses to allow her to take courses through the Bilingual Education Program, but I am not sure of their reasons. She seems to have very little content knowledge in the other subject areas, and I am concerned about how she will manage in the class.

Rassany is eager to please and is quite gregarious; she gets along well with both girls and boys in the class, and the other students like her, too. She can be disruptive during much of the day, since she does not follow directions or perhaps just doesn't understand them. Whatever the reason, she ends up talking to others, or making distracting noises to get attention during our lessons. There is a new district policy that requires me to place students below grade level in at least two subject areas in a special, pull-out program, and Rassany appears to be eligible for it. I am worried about three things: (1) her limited English language development, (2) her lack of content knowledge, and (3) moving her to a pull-out program after she has adjusted socially.

I have called her parents to set up a conference. They do not speak English and will need an interpreter for the meeting. I am not very optimistic about the meeting with them, especially since they cannot help her with homework.

Reflections and Observations: Rassany seems to be a social butterfly who can get along with others regardless of her language limitations. This is a positive characteristic. She may not be able to get help with reading English at home, but there are no details yet about home resources; maybe an older sister or friend or neighbor could help. She also seems adjusted to the class, even though she can be disruptive. The tone of the young teacher's remarks are supportive. She seems to want to keep Rassany in the class and is thinking about doing so to preserve the girl's social adjustment.

The teacher must weigh her choices carefully: Do Rassany's academic needs outweigh her social adjustment in class? And she must not assume that the conference with parents will not be useful just because an interpreter is needed—she must be patient and not make assumptions about what cannot be done, but think instead about what can be done under the circumstances. The teacher must investigate the bilingual program and the pull-out program to evaluate them against her own curriculum; perhaps she should consider coordinating her work with that of the specialists if Rassany or other children are referred for services.

It is still early in the year, which will work to the child's advantage if she must adjust to a new setting, as well as in her regular classroom. Children can be flexible and adjust well in two different learning environments if the adults manage the situation well and make the child comfortable in both settings.

Questions:

1. What are Rassany's current academic skills and talents?
2. What is best for Rassany's academic and social development?
3. How compatible are the bilingual and pull-out curricula with the curricula of the teacher?
4. Will a pull-out program negatively impact Rassany's relationships with her classmates?
5. Are there other children with similar academic profiles as Rassany's?
6. What diagnostic tools are normally used in the school to determine children's academic and social development?

Suggested Strategies:

- First, make more time to observe Rassany in class, and take a little time with her every week to get to know her better and to observe how she functions linguistically. Build a relationship so that you can learn firsthand about the child and collect more data on how she interacts with you and classmates. **(examining beliefs and knowledge about the child)** There are no facts to indicate that Rassany has been fully tested to discover all of her academic skills or the extent of her language development in English. All we know is that she can at least communicate with her English **and** Laotian speaking classmates. Have her tested so that you can understand what she knows and what she needs to work on. And try to find her teacher from last year to learn more about her academic growth over the last year.

- Second, the teacher can prepare her questions for the parents ahead of time, and send them to the interpreter. This will give the parents a chance to know her major concerns, and will ensure a productive meeting for all parties. **(thinking/planning ahead, honoring parent involvement)**

- Third, the teacher can call one of the bilingual teachers and the person responsible for the academic pull-out program, and ask for a joint meeting to learn as much as possible about each person's programs. **(using school resources/reviewing instructional practices)**

- Fourth, the teacher can explore the possibility of in-class assistance from the bilingual teacher if Rassany is allowed to stay in her class instead of joining the pull-out program. She can also ask why some parents do not enroll their children in the bilingual program and ask the bilingual teacher to refer her to some good references about the Laotian culture. **(building networks and resources)**

- Fifth, the teacher can call one of her friends from the university and ask her to do a search on refugee children's adjustment—especially Laotian—in schools after coming to the U.S. **(networking, beliefs and knowledge)**

- Sixth, the teacher can talk to her team leader to discuss the case, and find out if she can delay referring Rassany to the pull-out program. Finally, she can tell him she would like to brainstorm with someone in a similar situation, and perhaps work out a solution together. **(seeking dialogue with others)**

What are *your* suggested strategies for this scenario?

2.　1st Grade Pandemonium

It is the end of August, the end of the first day of class, and I have 25 new faces to learn to love. After 25 years, I still find the energy and excitement infectious. I like this classroom and I love my work. The aid who usually helps me is sick today, and the person sent to work with me has no experience with managing feisty first graders, so the little people take full advantage of her while I am greeting parents who have come to pick them up. It's OK, they are not too noisy, and are having fun getting to know each other after a full day of individual and group activities, including storytelling, skills tests, academic games, and recess. I usually spend the first day just getting to know the children through observations and interactions with them, and with their parents—during drop off and pick up.

These days the families are far different than they were when I first began. The neighborhood has changed and there are more poor families. School practices and laws have changed, so I now have to keep the special education children in class and the specialist comes in to help me with them and the others too. This sounds good. However, this summer bilingual education was voted out by the citizens, except in the most needy cases, and then it is limited to two years! I had thought seriously about retiring early, but so many people here depend on me. I am in charge of the elementary team to orient the new teachers, and I am responsible for staff development for the whole faculty. But lately I feel new myself, with all the changes, including new curricula, thanks to a rather conservative school board. I do want to stay to get my maximum benefits, so I guess I will stay for two more years.

Now that the last parent and child have left, I can settle down and read my notes, recall encounters with each child, and then scan their folders. Hmmmm, this year is going to be quite a challenge: There are more girls than boys and over half are from poor or dominated families.

- Five of my little ones are fluent in Spanish and English—3 girls, 2 boys.

- Three other girls speak Spanish, almost no English.

- Four Cambodian children have spoken very little, but seem to understand English enough to follow directions—2 girls, 2 boys.

- One boy with a speech impediment, a little shy, too.

- Two students, one boy, one girl, reading at the second grade level and they love to read.

- Five Black children who insisted on playing with each other and not with others—4 boys and 1 girl.

- One Irish immigrant girl who is a little withdrawn, and in the middle of her parent's international divorce—only the mother is allowed to drop her off and pick her up.

- A set of very friendly twin girls whose family strictly observes Kosher eating practices.

- One girl whose family lives in a shelter—they are on a waiting list for an apartment.

- One boy already diagnosed with Attention Deficit Disorder (ADD).

In one sense, these children are just an ordinary group of first graders. On the other hand, there are some serious challenges for me with those who may not be speaking English fluently, the ones with special circumstances—accelerated readers, speech impediment, and possibly the child with ADD; and a few with potential behavioral concerns—the child in the midst of the divorce, the children socialized to play only with each other.

Reflections and Observations:

This experienced teacher has some clear advantages in influencing the school climate as well as her classroom, through her role with new teachers and as staff developer for the whole faculty. All of the teachers are affected by the new curriculum, the new law on bilingual education, and the changing demographics in the neighborhood. She could take a leadership role and work out some details for her classroom simultaneously. It appears that her reputation is strong and positive since she has been selected for two such visible roles.

Her classroom cries out for a rich democratic theme based on the cultural diversity of the children, and this could tie in easily with the history of the country, no matter the curriculum. With what appears to be such a loving, caring attitude towards children, I bet she could model and teach cultural and racial tolerance along with demonstrating group interaction skills with academic and social lessons.

Continue the observation about how she can manage the diversity in her class. You might even want to list the type of diversity in her classroom.

Questions: List your questions here.

Suggested Strategies: Describe the strategies you would recommend.

3.   Mr. Martinez and Ms. McDonough

All the migrant eight graders were female this year. Fifteen of them! In this little town, their families picked apples and potatoes, and as the students got older, especially the girls, the families allowed them to remain on the mainland for the school year. Puerto Rico was home. The girls spoke English and Spanish, but their cognitive skills in English were not strong, and in the only middle school for miles around, Mr. Martinez was the only certified bilingual Spanish-English teacher. Maestro Juan Martinez was in his mid-thirties, studying for his doctorate at the local university, shy, and all business. He loved teaching, though, and math was his passion. He was respected, but he kept to himself and was perceived as a little mysterious. The students loved him, for though he was gentle, he pushed them hard and they excelled.

The class of girls was a little rambunctious, excited about staying on the mainland because they had made friends during the years they had come over for the migrant work, and they liked the States. They were poor, and the families they stayed with offered room and board, but no frills. Mr. Martinez knew that a few of them worked after school and cautioned them about not cutting into their study time.

Bilingual math is what they took from Mr. Martinez, who shared the use of a classroom once a week with another teacher who used the class four times a week. Ms. McDonough had been teaching mathematics for 17 years. In the middle school, she taught a basic course and two gifted seminars, and a new course on the Internet. Mr. Martinez's class met after one of her gifted seminars. She was not unfriendly, but she carried herself as if she owned the math department and the room they shared. She rarely had a good word for "those migrants who went back and forth all the time."

Last week Ms. McDonough approached Mr. Martinez to tell him that one of her students had his wallet containing 15 dollars stolen. She assured him rather emphatically that none of her students would ever do such a thing—they were not those kind of people, and besides, she wouldn't allow it. She asked him to check with his class and let her know right away if someone knew anything about it. Her tone was a bit condescending and intimidating, as usual. Mr. Martinez checked with his students and went back to tell her that his class knew nothing. She didn't believe him. They must know something—her students would never do anything like this! With this, she stormed past him, down to his classroom, and announced, "I know some of you had something to do with stealing that money, and you had better let me know about it before the end of the week!" Then she marched out, refusing to listen to reason from Mr. Martinez, who had run after her, only to get to the class at the end of her outburst.

The girls were very upset, some were crying, others withdrew and looked sullen. Others kept asking Mr. Martinez why Ms. McDonough hated them. They were scheduled to take her course as their first transition to an all-English mathematics class next term, and they were already threatening not to attend.

Mr. Martinez dismissed the class, feeling sick to his stomach. He told the girls he would do something, but he was upset, too, and uncertain about what he should do. McDonough was a bully, and she had no right to accuse the girls. No right, in fact, to come into the room after he had already asked the girls about the wallet. What a mess! He hated confrontations! "But she has insulted us all. I cannot let this pass . . . I must stand up for my students!"

Reflections and Observations: Note your observations here.

Questions: List your questions here.

Suggested Strategies: Describe the strategies you would recommend.

These scenarios have multiple issues to be addressed that challenge your competence in managing diversity along with other school problems. You have probably discovered that how you respond depends to a great extent on your experience, and, yes, your beliefs. When you share the scenarios with colleagues, you begin to understand how one scenario can take on so many meanings. Contributions from others broaden our horizons and stimulate new ideas. The pressures of the routine, tradition, policies, and structures of the school system influence us to acquiesce and think less about what is best for students, and more about what the system requires.

I believe it is very important for you to determine a process for managing the challenges that students with human differences present to you. What is the yardstick you will use to maintain the integrity of your vision about what schools are for and why you chose the profession? What is your gauge for determining whether you have made the right decision, or treated each student fairly? How far will you allow yourself to sink into groupthink and just do what everyone else does when controversies arise?

Well, you now have an opportunity to find out. Your homework in the last chapter is to develop an Action Plan to support the development of a student or group of students who are at risk of failing in your classroom or school. The challenge must be specific, and one for which you establish short-term and long-term goals. The Action Plan must be created in an area of interest to you, and one that will be of benefit to you and your colleagues. It can be a working, useful plan that can also benefit your district.

Summary Questions
Moving Toward Cultural Competence

A.	What evidence do I have that I am ready to be more reflective about my teaching and other professional behavior?
B.	What steps must I take to set the climate to accommodate children with human differences in my classroom?
C.	What is my vision for education today? Does it include the diversity of children who now represent our schools?
D.	What is the best way to engage my colleaugues in an effort to increase the achievement of our children at risk of educational failure?

Diversity Notebook

A. At the last faculty meeting, the middle school guidance counselor recommended that the school hold a forum for teachers and parents after several incidents of gay bashing were reported and an assault on two students who are believed to be gay took place. The recommendation was voted down because many teachers believe that the incidents were isolated, and no one was really hurt; other teachers expressed fears that such a forum would encourage students to "try homosexuality." You strongly believe a forum would reduce fears about homosexuality and educate the whole school community.

It is clear to you that student safety is an issue, even if this is the only incident to occur. Students unsure about their sexuality have confided in you about their fears of being hurt if it becomes known that they are confused or seeking counsel about the topic.

What are your next steps?

B. Can you identify the faculty in your school who have reputations as risk takers **and** strong advocates for children? You will need a team to help with your Action Plan, so begin to think about those folks who can help you.

References

Banks, J. A., & Banks, C. A. (1997). *Multicultural education.* Needham Heights, MA: Allyn & Bacon.

Gerloff, P. (1997). The power of self-connection: Transforming adults to reclaim the children. In J. T. Gibson (Ed.) *Educating the throwaway children* (p. 115). San Francisco: Jossey-Bass.

McDiarmid, G. W., & Price, J. (1993). Preparing teachers for diversity: A study of student teachers in a multicultural program. In M. J. O'Hara and S. J. Odell (Eds.), *Diversity and teaching.* Fort Worth: Harcourt Brace Jovanovich College.

Palmer, P. (1998). *The courage to teach.* San Francisco: Jossey-Bass.

CHAPTER 6

Planning for Diversity in Classrooms and Schools

In this last chapter the focus is on planning what educators must do to become more culturally competent. The goal of the planning is to gain experience in helping more diverse learners achieve at high levels. I hope the concepts and practices suggested, and the skills introduced, have stretched your thinking about how you can motivate and move all your current and future students to higher levels of learning. Making changes of the kind and magnitude that are required to assist students at risk of educational failure takes commitment, time, and energy, and therefore needs to be part of long-range planning in every school district. It takes time just to set the climate and bring a majority of the faculty and staff to a level of competence to work on systemic change. This can be done through establishing teams of educators and community people to work together to meet the goals. The teams can create innovative ways to meet the needs of diverse learners and then to integrate these strategies or programs so that they benefit all learners.

Long-term planning using teams has been the experience of a school district in Delaware that has been using, revising, and evaluating their Team Approach to Mastery (TAM) since 1975, when they first tried inclusion. They began moving the special needs children from resource rooms into the regular classes; their plan for the future was to eliminate the resource rooms entirely. Today, the district has no more resource rooms, but over 100 TAM classrooms serving children from ages 3 to 21, with a ratio of two nondisabled children to each child with a disability. Their progress and success evolved steadily due to a deliberate planning process that has been evaluated on a continuous basis throughout the years.

What is impressive to me is the simplicity of their model, which uses components similar to the framework described in this book. Their framework had several components, including: (1) *teacher collaboration*—called teacher cadres; they work together through release time twice a month and collaborate with other teachers in their classrooms. They work not just to enhance the achievement of the children who are at risk, but on an integrated pedagogy for all children; (2) *program evaluation*—they monitor the work of disabled and nondisabled children and use the feedback to revise and reorganize as necessary, or reinforce current activity as the results indicate; and (3) *staff development*—a component absolutely necessary to the success of their program. The growth and development of all instructors and administrators are grounded in learning from each other through a formal staff development process. It was not a miracle. They made it happen by working together, taking risks, learning from each other and from the children. Their plan was realized after several years of experimenting, making mistakes, learning from them, and watching children progress and benefit academically and socially from their efforts.

Sooner or later every American school system will have to plan for diversity of one kind or another. For many educators, the need for planning has already arrived, and still others have been involved in the process for some time. The earlier chapters have discussed some of the threats to the academic success of children who represent a variety of human differences that neither schools nor our society are well equipped to manage. The social, economic, and political conditions of our society are reflected in the schools. If gender diversity and the lag in accomplishment for girls in the sciences is at issue in schools, then there is a similar problem in the general society—a dearth of women in the scientific fields. If the safety of children with a different sexual orientation is an issue in schools, it is likely to be an issue in our general society—hence the use of civil rights laws already passed to protect these citizens, too. If discrimination based on race, culture, or religion is evident in school programs, chances are pretty good that these issues are serious ones in the larger society. My point is this: We adults, inside and outside of schools, have a shared responsibility to provide each child with the best educational experience possible for his or her own development and to be a valuable, contributing member of our society. In our society, our micro-cultures overlap and we ultimately feel (as a society) the effects of those who are not valued if we do not do something to improve the odds for their success and participation in this pluralistic culture.

To reduce the problems with children at risk of failing, or to establish a preventive program for those potentially vulnerable to failing, I am proposing that you prepare an Action Plan. Why an Action Plan? Creating one will provide a way for you to practice your increasing cultural competence and move your class, school, or district forward in working more effectively with students who need your assistance. You will have to decide on the human difference or the type of diversity you want to address. Here are some of the categories of diversity described in earlier chapters, as well as some of their major problems:

- children with mental or physical impairments/low expectations/intelligence questioned
- children with accelerated or exceptional talents/no special programs for development/bored to distraction
- second language learners/not learning content in bilingual programs/low expectations
- children of different races and cultures/low expectations/intelligence questioned
- children who are homosexual or think they may be/lives in danger/no counseling
- children with behavioral problems/ineffective management/low expectations
- middle school girls/low expectations in science and math/low confidence
- poor children/low expectations/intelligence questioned

This list is not exhaustive and may not cover the diversity in your classroom or school. Any human difference that places a child at risk of not progressing academically can be a part of your Action Plan. You can choose a child who is absent often, one who is ostracized because of her religion, or one who shows signs of being shunned and is a behavior problem at school. Often there are larger concerns, such as social isolation, that may be the underlying cause of school problems.

There are few short-term answers, and many of these conditions cannot be remedied by educators alone. Collaboration and support from families and personnel at community agencies may be necessary to realize short- and long-term solutions. Long-term planning will be necessary to meet some of the challenges presented by children in at-risk situations. Involving children as part of the planning may be necessary to learn more about meeting some of their needs. For example, if teachers are planning courses specifically to attract girls to the sciences, they might consult girls about how they would respond to certain aspects of the plan in a brainstorming session. Students who have experienced discrimination can contribute to creating a fair code of conduct for all to maintain.

There are no magic solutions, but there are programs that work. Changes in attitude and behavior could introduce a climate of respect and fairness that could signal a positive change for all students, not just those at risk of failing. For example, how students are welcomed at school and how well they are treated can be a strong beginning that will lead to academic recovery. How they are taught (not always teacher centered, or lectures) and what they are taught (some inclusive curricula that include people with disabilities and members of dominated groups) can empower or disempower students. Curriculum influences whether they will be respected, tolerated, or ignored, which makes a difference in how they feel about themselves and the school.

Confidence-building activities can motivate students as much as adult modeling of how to handle conflict and violence effectively. Creating an atmosphere that Roland Barth (1996, Virginia Biggy lecture at UMass Lowell) describes as a *community of learners* where everyone is learning—the principal, teachers, specialists, and of course children—would also make school a very attractive place for all children. A middle school principal and her staff discovered the meaning of this phrase, a community of learners, as they attempted to reduce the number of girls and boys in their school who join gangs.

The gang membership was increasing in this Texas middle school of predominately Hispanic youngsters, despite the banning of colors and other gang symbols. Girls and boys admired gang members, especially the ones in high school, while others were actually members at the middle school. It was difficult for many of these children to view school as an ally when the majority of them were labeled failures—and had the Fs to prove it. Repeated failures and poor grades were driving children to gangs and placing them at risk in a setting where they knew they were supposed to achieve. Students' self-identity took a psychological beating every day in school, yet they gladly endured real hazing and beatings when they were part of the rites that initiated them into gang membership.

Asked about how he could join a gang and endure such violence, one youngster replied to the principal, "We protect each other, Miss. We're family. . . . In school we are 'nothings.' In a gang, we are somebodies" (Juarez, 1996, p. 30). Determined to engineer academic success, build a stronger sense of self for the children, and promote a different learning environment for teachers and students, the principal and her staff researched successful programs for similar students, and learned that with changes in schools and joint alliances with strong neighbor-based programs, they had a chance at meeting their goals. Working with students, staff, and community organizations and leaders, these teams did the following:

- organized a variety of special clubs (almost 50)—academic, recreational, international, musical—to attract students back to school
- recruited community volunteers from lay and professional organizations to mentor, tutor, and befriend children
- broadened instructional work to become more activity based— using hands-on work, and other commercial reading materials in addition to the text
- abolished the grade of F (which was such a powerful stigma for children), and replaced the F with a grade of I, which meant incomplete with more time to complete their work
- extended the school year, thereby offering students more time to learn. (pp. 31–31)

Their work together brought many positive changes. Truancy and dropout rates were reduced significantly; students' life aspirations were influenced by mentors, making gang membership much less attractive; teachers and students learned more about each other; and school became a fun place to be. Most important, some students were experiencing academic success for the first time. Systemic changes such as the extended year and grading were tough obstacles, yet were ultimately overcome because a whole community knew the lives of children were at stake; and they chose to make the investment in change for the whole school. These kinds of transformations require your commitment, time, and energy, and yet the benefits are enormous for everybody. Are you ready to make a change for your children at risk of educational failure?

Getting Started

First, you have to decide which topic you want to pursue. Think of a problem you want to solve that is related to a selected population at risk of educational failure. State the problem in question form and then work from there to the next step. Here are some sample questions:

A.   How do we get more middle school girls interested in chemistry? The actual plan may include an increase of a specific number of girls in chemistry by the year 2000. You may need to start with introducing chemistry to girls through experiments and workshops in elementary school!

B.   Why are so many African American boys in elementary school disciplined more than other children? Your goal might be to reduce the number by the end of the year (to increase the number who graduate to middle school) and then continue to decrease the number each year until there is no longer a problem. You might have to investigate racial attitudes toward African Americans, or how discipline is managed by teachers, or both.

C.   Why do most of the Spanish speaking, middle school bilingual children have trouble with content knowledge after transfer to mainstream classes? The goal may be to reduce the grade level performance gap between the Spanish speaking children and the English speakers before they enter middle school. Learning about how the bilingual program works and how the teachers manage the transition will assist you in meeting your goal.

Final titles can look like this: An Action Plan to Increase the Enrollment of Girls in Chemistry by 20% in the Class of 2000; An Action Plan to Reduce the Number of African American Elementary Boys Referred for Disciplinary Action by Half by the End of the School Year 1999; An Action Plan to Develop a Peer Mediation Program for Controlling Anger in the Marshall Elementary School; An Action Plan to Increase the Content Knowledge to Grade Level of all Mainstreamed Spanish Bilingual Sixth Graders by the 2000.

Understanding how to define and state a problem is important. Notice that each question names a specific group, grade level, and has an academic or social goal related to school. Now that you have chosen a topic, organize a team to work with you, selecting people interested in the topic, as well as some who have experienced success working with the target group or with some aspect of the problem. Start with a small group of three or four; you can always add a few people as the need arises for different talents.

The school improvement literature indicates that having some defined team roles can enhance your work. Eisenman and Fleming (1989) offer these roles as important ones: (1) *Champions*, who serve as advocates for the proposed improvement; (2) *Context Analyzers*, who must be able to interpret what the local issues are that can affect the changes, including knowing district priorities, local politics, faculty interests, and the like; (3) *Coordinators and Communicators*, who must work among all constituents to ensure that information is received and shared on a regular basis, and also work among and between constituents affected by the improvement; (4) *Support Providers*, who handle a variety of logistical, psychological, and instructional support; and (5) *Implement Monitors,* who are folks who work with everyone to ensure that all aspects of the improvement plan become operational, including monitoring follow-up (p. 5). You may find other roles, as well, but the make-up of your team is worth discussing and it is important to place appropriate people in the right roles.

Next, you need to decide on your collaborators outside the team. These people may include faculty and staff at other school sites or local community people from institutions and businesses. You will want to contact collaborators soon after you have defined the population you want to work with and begin to engage them in the planning process. Doing your homework about who they are and understanding their positions and interests will provide a strong basis for collaboration and partnership. They are more likely to listen and learn from you when they know you have taken the time to understand them.

Now you need to determine how much research you need to do to develop a challenging but realistic plan. This requires that you develop an outline of what areas you want to explore in answering the questions you posed to meet the goal of your plan. After making an outline, you can think through each part and determine what type of information you need. Here is a list of general functions your plan should cover: (1) define the problem and include some evidence that it actually exists, (2) present the background of the problem and the current status of the problem at the selected site, (3) identify and discuss research by other professionals who have addressed the problem, and/or identify programs or activities that others (local, regional or national) have used to successfully address the problem, if available, (4) discuss how your plan is similar or different from the research and existing programs, and (5) recommend strategies to rectify, reduce, or resolve the problem in your classroom or school.

The final steps are assigning tasks and developing a realistic timetable for accomplishing each task. Envision specific roles needed to complete your tasks, then work on assigning team members who have the skills to fit particular roles. This might mean recruiting more people; just be certain that there is a consensus that you need the role and the extra individual. You and your team members can find resources in the school—people (including students) knowledgeable about your topic, as well as documents and records of many varieties. There are also the more traditional resources such as the library, and new ones such as the Internet, to support your work.

I urge you to use the framework described earlier as a guide in developing your plan. Using the four lenses—reflecting about *your* pedagogical practices, examining *your* beliefs and knowledge about diverse groups, understanding the change process and building networks of resources *inside*—influences you to first look inward at yourselves, and then facilitates your moving outward—to other people and resources. I believe it is very important to make time to allow the team to build its relationships, until there is full understanding and consensus about their roles and the need for such a plan.

Parker Palmer's (1998) words about a teacher's authority are encouraging, especially when we encounter those outside who always have a better way for us to do our work:

> External tools of power have occasional utility in teaching, but they are no substitute for authority, the authority that comes from the teacher's inner life. The clue is in the word itself, which has *author* at its core. Authority is granted to people who are perceived as *authoring* their own words, their own actions, their own lives, rather than playing a scripted role at great remove from their own hearts. (p. 33)

This reminds us that we are at our core teachers who must work at building successful experiences for all our students. We must first recognize and rely on our own authority and the validity of our own vision before we seek the counsel of others. The suggestions for the Action Plan will assist in the outward search, which will complement the authority established within.

Resource

Center for Research on Education, Diversity and Excellence (CREDE). CREDE is a national research and development center operated under a cooperative agreement between the University of California, Santa Cruz, and the Office of Educational Research and Improvement (OERI) of the U.S. Department of Education.

The overall mission of CREDE is to assist the nation's population of diverse students, including those at risk of educational failure, to achieve to high academic standards. To accomplish this, CREDE does the following: (1) designs, develops, and disseminates a comprehensive framework for educational systems that is strong, flexible, and inclusive for diversity among all individuals and communities; (2) conducts research with concrete connections to practice to discover, develop, and disseminate fundamental knowledge about the ways that diverse at-risk students can attain excellence in education.

CREDE addresses educational excellence from preschool to higher education for students from all major linguistic, cultural, and ethnic groups, including those suffering all four identified risk factors for educational failure—limited English proficiency, poverty/economic disadvantage, race, and geographic location. After years of research, reviews of the literature, and study of model school programs, CREDE has identified five principles based on their consistent findings and on strong consensus from the field. These principles are important for all children, but are vital for children at risk of educational failure, and will be use as an organizing structure in the implementation of programs for them:

Principle 1: Facilitate learning through joint productive activity among teachers and students.

Principle 2: Develop competence in the language and literacy of instruction throughout all instructional activities.

Principle 3: Contextualize teaching and curriculum in the experiences and skills of home and community.

Principle 4: Challenge students toward cognitive complexity.

Principle 5: Engage students through dialogue, especially the instructional conversation.

Details of the principles and information on their research projects and programs can be found by contacting CREDE at 1156 High Street, Santa Cruz, California 95064. Telephone: 408-459-3500; Fax: 408-44459-3502; E-mail crede@cats.ucsc.edu; www.cal.org/crede

References

Eiseman, J. W., & Fleming, D. S. (1989). *The role of teams in implementing school improvement plans.* Andover, MA: The Regional Laboratory.

Juarez, T. (1996). Where homeboys feel at home in school. *Educational Leadership, 53*(5), 30–32.

Palmer, P. (1998). *The courage to teach.* San Francisco: Jossey-Bass.

Author Index

A

Apple, M., 11
Ashton, P., 73

B

Banks, C. A., 19, 84
Banks, J. A., 19, 84
Barth, R., 104
Beane, J. A., 11
Berla, N., 51
Berman, P., 37
Binet, Alfred, 64
Boyer, E., 48

C

Carr, J., 41
Checkley, 66
Collins, Marva, 31, 40
Comer, J. P., 30, 40
Crandall, 37

D

Darling-Hammond, L., 46, 48
Detterman, D. K., 30, 65
Dewey, John, 11
Doda, N. A., 73
Ducette, J. P., 66

E

Epstein, Joyce, 23, 30

F

Fleming, D. S., 107
Fletcher, S., 74
Fuerstein, R., 30
Fullan, Michael, 37, 39, 47–48, 49, 50

G

Gardner, Howard, 30, 66, 67
Gerloff, Pamela, 83
Gibson, S., 74
Goodlad, J., 11, 48

H

Haberman, M., xi
Hall, G. E., 37
Hargreaves, A., 48
Henderson, A. T., 23, 51
Hirsh, S., 37
Hord, S. M., 37
Howard, J., 8, 75–76

J

Juarez, T., 105

K

Kamii, Constance, 63
Kohl, Herbert, 73

L

Levin, Hank, 31, 40
Levine, M., xii, 25–27, 40, 81
Loucks-Horsley, S., 37, 39

M

McDiarmid, G. W., 87
McLaughlin, M., 37, 46
Meier, Deborah, 31, 39

N

Negroni, Peter, 8

O

Omotani, L. M., 73

P

Palmer, Parker, 83, 109
Powell, Richard R., 23, 24, 25, 40, 87
Price, J., 87

R

Rist, R. C., 75
Roberts, J. I., 19, 20, 22
Rokeach, M., 41
Rosenthal, R., 75

S

Sarason, S. B., 48
Schaefer, R. T., 18, 22
Schon, Donald, 44, 45
Senge, P., 49
Sewell, T. E., 66
Shapiro, J. P., 66
Sizer, Ted, 31
Soder, R., 11
Sparks, D., 37
Spearman, C., 65
Spring, J., 22
Sternberg, Robert, 30, 65, 67, 68–69
Stiegelbauer, S., 39

T

Tatum Berverly Daniels, 42
Thurstone, L. L., 65
Tracz, S. M., 72

V

Vygotsky, L. S., 30

W

Webb, R. B., 73
Weber, B. J., 73
Wellman, D., 42
Wolcott, Harry, 18, 19

Z

Zeigler, S., 50

SUBJECT INDEX

A

Academic achievement of American
children, 47
Acculturation, 18
Achievement tests, 62–64
Action Plan, 97–98, 103–104, 107
Assessment of children as learners, 10
Attention Deficit Disorder (ADD), 59, 64

B

Building resources for networking, 88

C

California Achievement Test, 62
Center for Research on Education,
Diversity and Excellence (CREDE),
109–110
Center on Families, Community Schools
and Children's Learning, 51
Change Forces (Fullan), 39, 48
*Change in Schools, Facilitating the
Process* (Hall and Hord), 37
Change process, 35–37
national models, 39–40
and staff development, 37–39
teacher's change strategy, 40–52
understanding, 87–88
Civil Rights Movement, 23
Collaboration, 108
with community, 51, 104
with families, 104
among teachers, 46, 49–50, 86
Community, collaboration with, 51, 104
Community of learners, 104
Compulsory educational laws, 17
Concerns-Based Adoption Model
(C-BAM), 37–39, 88
Confidence-building activities, 104–106
Courage to Teach, The (Palmer), 83
Cultural domain, 17, 19
dominant, 19
primary, 20
Cultural pluralism, 18
Cultural world view, 17
Culture, defined, 18, 19–20
Curriculum
inclusive, 104
reshaping, 24

D

Democracy, Education and the Schools
(Soder), 11
Democratic schools, 11–12
Discipline of Hope, The (Kohl), 73
Diversity
and achievement, 59–60
and culture, 17–33
defined, 1–7
issues, 5–6
planning for, 101–110

E

Educational care, 26, 81
*Educational Care: A System for Under-
standing and Helping Children
with Learning Problems at Home
and in School* (Levine), xii, 26
Educational reform, 10–11
*Education Reforms and Students At Risk:
A Review of the Current State of
the Art,* 8–10
Efficacy, of teachers, 73–74
Efficacy Institute, 75, 77
Efficacy Model of Development, 77
English language learners, 10
Examining beliefs and knowledge of
diverse groups, 87
Expectation, teacher, 75–78

F

Families
as conveyors of culture, 28
networking with, 50–52
teacher's interaction with, 29–30

H

Holmes Report, 1995, 47
Human differences, 7–8
reactions to, 8

I

Inquiry, 49
Intelligence
assessing, 59–62
beliefs about, 30–31
defining, 64–69
multiple, 30

ABOUT THE AUTHOR

Dr. Joyce Taylor Gibson, Associate Professor of Education at the University of Massachusetts Lowell, has been a teacher educator for over a decade. In 1997 her peers at the College of Education selected her as the recipient of the First Faculty Teaching award. Joyce is also the Coordinator of the Family School Partnership Project, an action-research initiative that seeks to strengthen relationships between school personnel and families to foster greater achievement in children. Her recently edited book, *Educating the Throwaway Children: What We Can Do to Help Children at Risk,* offers new strategies and insights from educators who have been successful working with children at risk of educational failure. Joyce is a Southerner who received her Ph.D. from the University of Florida.